CREATING AN ANTIQUE LOOK IN HAND-HOOKED RUGS

Happy Hooking!

Gail Horn

CREATING AN ANTIQUE LOOK IN HAND-HOOKED RUGS

CYNTHIA SMESNY NORWOOD

Virginia P. Stimmel, Editor
photographs by Bill Bishop/Impact Xpozures

DEDICATION

This book is dedicated to all the rug hookers I have been lucky enough to meet since 1980. I can't imagine what my life would be without those special friendships. Thank you for crossing my path.

Published by
STACKPOLE BOOKS
5067 Ritter Road
Mechanicsburg, PA 17055
www.stackpolebooks.com

Printed in China

First edition

10 9 8 7 6 5 4 3 2 1

Cover photos by Bill Bishop/Impact Xpozures
Cover design by Caroline Stover

Library of Congress Cataloging-in-Publication Data

Frontispiece: Tulip Cross by Katie Hartner

Creating An Antique Look In Hand-Hooked Rugs / Virginia P. Stimmel, editor; photographs by Bill Bishop.—1st ed.
    p. cm.

  ISBN: 1-881982-59-9;
  978-1-881982-59-3
Canadian GST #R137954772.

CONTENTS

About the Author viii

Introduction ix

From the Editor 1

About the Publisher 1

CHAPTER 1   Basic Elements of the Antique Look..................................2
Design
Width of Cut
Color

CHAPTER 2   Designs and Patterns 6
Using Commercial Patterns
Designing Your Own Patterns
Choosing a Backing or Foundation
Transferring Your Own Designs
Copyright

CHAPTER 3   Color..18
Color Theory
Color Planning for an Antique Look

CHAPTER 4   Width of Cuts and Hook Sizes 29
Cutting Your Wool
Choosing a Hook

CHAPTER 5   Hooking the Main Design..................................35

CHAPTER 6   Hooking the Background 38
Color: Light, Medium, or Dark?
Hooking Style
Echo
Halo
Blocking
Random
S Shape
Hit and Miss
Mixtures
Background Tips
A Word about Borders

CHAPTER 7   Specialty Fabrics 48
Recycled Fabrics
Preparing Recycled Fabrics
Testing Recycled Wool
Vintage Fabrics
Fashion or Designer Fabrics

CHAPTER 8   Finishing Methods..55
The Importance of Steaming
Historical Methods of Finishing
Current Recommendations
My Favorite Finishing Methods
Labeling

CHAPTER 9   Dyeing Techniques for an Antique Look 62
Basic Guidelines
Onion Skins
Walnut Hulls
Marrying or Stewing Fabrics
Removing Color
Chemical Dyes
Dyeing Tips
My Favorite Dye Formulas

CHAPTER 10   Breaking the Rules...71

CHAPTER 11   Free Pattern with Suggestions and Photos...........73

CHAPTER 12   How to Hook..75

About the Magazine 77
Resources 78

ACKNOWLEDGEMENT

While there are many people to thank for their input in conjunction with this book, several must be mentioned by name: Barbara Carroll who opened her house and heart so that many great antique rugs could be shared with others; Laurice Heath who in changing her life, opened this door for me; Ginny Stimmel, Editor of Rug Hooking magazine, who walked me through deadlines, publishing terms, and learning curves; to those in this book who graciously said yes when I asked to borrow or photograph a rug; to all the great teachers I have been exposed to including Emma Lou Lais, Barbara Carroll, Jule Marie Smith, Pat Chancey, Jackye Hansen, Betty Krull, Joyce Krueger, Diane Stoffel, D. Marie Bresch, Jane Olson, and yes, the list could just keep going, but I must stop somewhere. One more person finishes the list of those who must be acknowledged—Larry Norwood. He never sees the mess, the wool fuzz balls, piles of wool and paisleys, or complains about the travel, but most importantly, he finds value in my work. I hope for all rug hookers to find the same contentment in their endeavors.

ABOUT THE AUTHOR

Cynthia Smesny Norwood, a native of Texas, started hooking rugs in 1980. Her first exposure to rug hooking came after she and her husband moved to northeastern Ohio. She saw samples of the craft at the Apple Butter Festival in Burton, Ohio, and she was "hooked." Although she has a BA in history and English, her first love has always been art. Her first hooking projects were #3-cuts—flowers, birds, and Orientals—but that wasn't exactly what she was looking for. Then she discovered a simpler pattern in which she used mainly recycled gray-brown herringbone, with a little peach for color, and hooked it in a wider cut. Like the work of most artists, hers continued to evolve, becoming more primitive and finally acquiring an antique look.

Cynthia Smesny Norwood is codirector of Star of Texas Rug Camp in Fredericksburg, Texas; director of Cross Creek Rug Camp in Newbury, Ohio; and founder and director of Winedale Rug Hooking Retreat, Round Top, Texas, for the University of Texas American Historical Studies Center. She is a past board member and current advertising manager of the Association of Traditional Hooking Artists (ATHA) and a McGown certified teacher. She has exhibited at the Museum of American Decorative Arts in Houston and at the Clear Lake Arts Alliance in Houston, Texas. Awards include best of show and second and third place at the Geauga County (Ohio) Fair, as well as second place from the Victoria Arts Council. Cynthia has participated in *Rug Hooking* magazine's *Celebration of Hand-Hooked Rugs* II, III, IX, XI, and XII and was a past judge for *Celebration XV*. She has written articles for *Rug Hooking* magazine and ATHA's newsletter. She was the 1997 visiting artist at the Southwest Arts and Craft Center, San Antonio, Texas, and chairperson of the 1995 ATHA Biennial celebration and co-chairman of the 2007 ATHA Biennial in New Orleans, Louisiana. She has taught workshops across the United States and currently teaches private workshops in her home in Kirtland, Ohio.

Horse, 47¹/₂" x 30". This may be a Robert Sands Frost pattern. Note the limited use of color and the directional hooking in the background. Chestnuts and walnuts may have provided dye for the background. The horse's legs fade into the ground, but they're not lost because of the color of the hooves. The softness of this piece, the wonderful hooking techniques used in the background, the simplicity of the scroll, and the pride of the horse make this one of my favorites. (From the Barbara Carroll Collection.)

INTRODUCTION

Rug hooking has enjoyed a burst of popularity in the last ten years, particularly the style known as "primitive." Basically, a primitive rug has a simple design or theme, incorporates interesting textures and unusual uses of color, and has no concern about the lack of proportion, perspective, or balance. The next most popular category of hooked rugs is the "antique-looking" style. This group is made up mainly of the primitive rugs but also includes florals, geometrics, and pictorials. This book focuses on creating an antique-looking rug that has all the best qualities of a new rug.

Kinderhook Flower Basket, 23" x 33". This antique rug, hooked in about 1920 or earlier, breaks one of the main rules of color: the sassy red is used only in the center and nowhere else. The basket also appears to be floating—it's not resting on a table, it's just there. This technique is common in antique and antique-looking rugs. Also note the imperfections of the basket and how the bouquet overlaps the borderlines on one side but not the other. This is a fabulous soft, warm rug. (Original from the Barbara Carroll Collection. Printed by Woolley Fox in the *Keeping the Past Alive* series.)

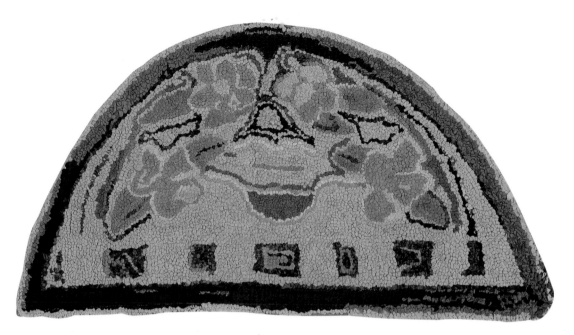

The two main reasons for the popularity of antique-looking rugs are decor and time. This style works well in any room and in any type of home; an antique-looking rug adds warmth to any decor. But more than likely, the time factor is the real reason for the popularity of this style. Achieving this antique look involves the use of "as-is" wools (fabrics that don't need to be dyed) as well as a much wider cut of wool. Both steps save time and allow artists to concentrate on the actual hooking process. Thus, rug hookers are more quickly rewarded with finished pieces to enjoy. They can express themselves through the beauty of their rugs while creating something functional at the same time.

Before starting your own antique creation, study collections of antique rugs, photographs, exhibits, and rug designers' catalogs. Focus on the common elements that appeal to your sense of style. Let your likes and preferences guide the type of rug you decide to hook. Don't hook a star simply because everyone else is hooking them. Take the time to create an antique rug that is truly yours, whether you use a commercial pattern or your own design. Feel free to break some of the rules you learned about color and technique. This book will help you express your sense of style and create a unique antique-looking hooked rug that can be enjoyed by future generations.

Antique Bowl of Flowers, 33" x 17". This charming, cozy antique rug breaks many rules. By most standards, the top is too "heavy" for the rest of the rug. The bowl is just floating, and the flowers don't appear to be connected to it. The soft pinks are used only in the flowers. I like how the outside border has faded into different values, but I particularly love the fact that I don't know what's going on in the small squares at the base of the rug. It could be letters or just nonsense, but it definitely caught my attention. (From the author's collection.)

New York Geometric, 33" x 20". Probably hooked in about 1885, this antique rug contains only about 25 percent wool; the rest is mainly dress silks. Although the palette is soft, the use of the strong black line is not offensive. The single red line around the outside edge of the border gives this rug even more interest. (Original from the Barbara Carroll Collection. Printed by Woolley Fox in the *Keeping the Past Alive* series.)

FROM THE EDITOR

Hooked rugs, considered to be America's one indigenous folk art, first appeared in the eighteenth century in Atlantic Canada and New England. At that time our predecessors used any materials they had on hand—old clothing, blankets, feed sacks—to create rugs to cover their bare floors. Most designs were uncomplicated and primitive—proportion and perspective were often disregarded.

One of the most popular requests of rug hookers today is how to achieve the antique look in hand-hooked rugs. Nothing beats the beauty of an antique rug—the faded patina, the arrangement of the simple designs, and the charm of the seemingly random placement of color. Author Cynthia Norwood breaks down the process with easy-to-follow information plus tips and recommendations on how to achieve your goal. She will lead you through the study of common elements in antique hooked rugs to create your own pattern from start to finish—transferring, customizing, color planning, dyeing techniques, and which cuts of wool work best. Everything you need to know about different background treatments and fabric use is included—medium versus light or dark and what effect the background has on the finished product.

For a good look at what rug hookers are doing with yesteryear's craft, pick up a copy of *Rug Hooking* magazine, or visit our web site at *www.rughookingmagazine.com*. Within the world of rug hooking and *Rug Hooking* magazine, you'll find a style to suit every taste and a growing community of giving, gracious fiber artists who will welcome you to their gatherings.

—Ginny Stimmel

ABOUT THE PUBLISHER

Rug Hooking magazine welcomes you to the rug hooking community. Since 1989 *Rug Hooking* has served thousands of rug hookers around the world with its instructional, illustrated articles on dyeing, designing, color planning, hooking techniques, and more. Each issue of the magazine contains color photographs of beautiful rugs old and new, profiles of teachers, designers, and fellow rug hookers, and announcements of workshops, exhibits, and gatherings.

Rug Hooking has responded to its readers' demands for more inspiration and information by establishing an inviting, informative website at *www.rughookingmagazine.com* and by publishing a number of books on this fiber art. Along with how-to pattern books, *Rug Hooking* has produced the competition-based book series *Celebration of Hand-Hooked Rugs*, now in its 18th year.

The hand-hooked rugs you'll see in *Celebration of Hand-Hooked Rugs XVII* represent just a fragment of the incredible art that is being produced today by women and men of all ages. For more information on rug hooking and *Rug Hooking* magazine, call or write to us at the address on the copyright page.

CHAPTER 1

Basic Elements of the Antique Look

Three major elements are fundamental to creating an antique look in a hooked rug:
- Design
- Width of cut
- Color.

DESIGN

Simplicity is the key when designing an antique-looking rug. The basic design can range from flowers to geometrics to pictorials to simple objects, but it must not be intricate or complicated by excessive detail. Simplicity equals pleasure to the eye of the observer. Choose a subject that appeals to your own sense of style or your personal taste. These rugs should be individual and exclusive, because they are the antiques of the future.

You don't need to be an artist to draw your own pattern, because proportion and scale aren't important. It doesn't really matter that the dog is twice the size of the tree. If the dog is more important than the tree, wouldn't it be larger in the designer's mind? Even if you're hooking

Original Tennessee Hearts, 35" x 39". This wonderful rug is made of only 25 percent wool; it also contains dress silks and cotton. The use of red is fabulous because it is bright and flashy, is used sporadically, and keeps the eye moving. Note that the hearts aren't perfect, and the corner hearts aren't spaced accurately from the center heart. (Original from the Barbara Carroll Collection. Printed by Woolley Fox in the *Keeping the Past Alive* series.)

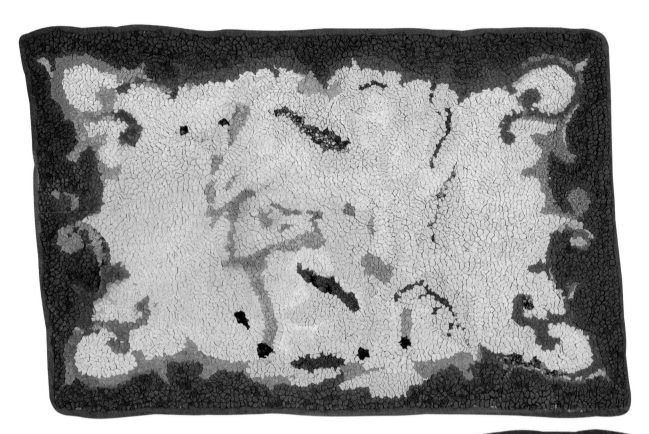

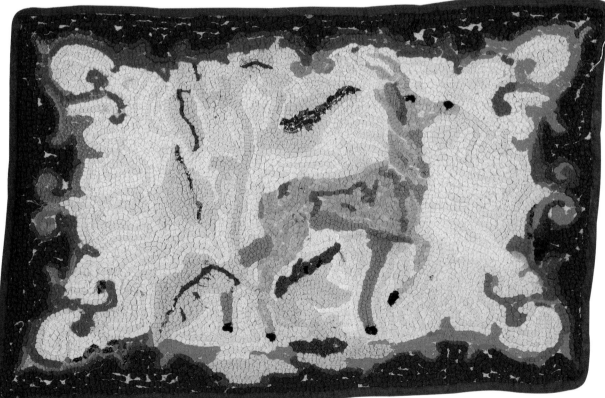

Antique Faded Deer, 34" x 24". The deer facing to the left is the correct side of this rug. When you look at the reverse side, you can see how much the rug has faded. The softness of the tree-shaped image makes you wonder what the original color looked like. Note the red scroll used around the border but nowhere else. This prancing deer was hooked with wool and cotton. In primitive hooked rugs, you should be able to see some of the burlap or linen on the reverse side—if you don't, the rug is hooked too tightly. (From the author's collection.)

1790 Eagle, 37" x 25". Designed by Edith O'Neal. Hooked by Charlotte Allison of Frederickburg, Texas. By using a medium-value background, Charlotte instantly aged this rug. She also used several values of the same color in the background. The quirkiness of the stars gives the rug more personality; it would have been boring had each star been the same. The eagle almost fades into the background, but his crest ensures that you don't lose him.

Antique Ligonier Duo, 43" x 29". This antique, owned by Barbara Carroll of Ligonier, Pennsylvania, was hooked in about 1885 with dress silks. The glow around the cats sets them apart from the multiple backgrounds. (Printed by Woolley Fox in the *Keeping the Past Alive* series.)

Ligonier Duo, 30" x 19". Hooked by Jane Hester of Kinderhook, New York. This was the first new *Ligonier Duo* to be hooked. It has a wonderful soft, old look, and the soft reds used in the flowers are pleasing. (Available through Woolley Fox.)

Ligonier Duo, 42" x 28". Hooked by Lois Lee Ewing of Kerrville, Texas—a larger version hooked with a #9-cut on linen. Note the use of reds, especially on the toes. Lois broke one of the rules by hooking that big block of off-white right in the center. It certainly draws your eye away from the border and to the important items—the cats. (Available through Woolley Fox.)

a commercial pattern, you can make changes—simply leave something out or draw one of the items larger than the original. Give the pattern your own personal touch, and make it one of a kind.

WIDTH OF CUT

The width of the wool strips can vary greatly, but for an antique-looking rug, think wider. Our ancestors didn't have Fraser, Bliss, Rigby, or Townsend machines to make the cutting easy and uniform. Tearing the strips or cutting them with scissors was their only means of strip making. Just imagine how much easier it would be to hand-cut a #8-cut ($^8/_{32}$") versus a #3-cut ($^3/_{32}$"). And if you were hand-cutting, it would be impossible to create identical strips. So feel free to use a cutter, but vary the width of the strips. On some cutters, you can simply move the guide; on others, you need to change the size of the

cutter head. For more variety, you can also mix hand-cut or torn strips with machine-cut strips. Don't be concerned about mixing different cuts; this will just add to the unique look. I usually use Townsend #9 and #10 mixed with torn strips, but I completed one rug using Rigby cuts #3 through #8 because I was trying to use up all the leftover strips. When mixing strips of different widths, you'll achieve the best look if you pull all the cuts as high as you pull the widest strip.

COLOR

The most important aspect of creating an antique-looking rug is color and the way it is used. You might think that this would be the easiest part—just use dull, dead, drab colors. But you would be wrong. I have seen some great designs hooked with only dull colors, and the result was heartbreaking. The rug didn't sing or even talk

Ligonier Duo, 30" x 19". Hooked by Cynthia Norwood of Kirtland, Ohio, with a #9-cut on linen. The red cats glow faintly but are softened by the assortment of greens. Many different paisleys were used, mainly in the flowers and cats. Even the stems of the flowers are antique paisley. (Pattern available through Woolley Fox. Paisleys available through Cynthia Norwood.)

to the brain; it had no life or personality. You don't want to waste your valuable time creating a lifeless rug. The antique rugs we enjoy today didn't start out with that aged, mellow look; it evolved over time due to wear and exposure to light. Look at the reverse side of an antique rug. Even if the original colors were grays and browns, you'll see that they are much more vibrant on the back of the rug. You can easily see which colors faded the most—normally, blues and blue-greens lose their intensity first.

The colors you choose should be full of life, but subtle. Most of the color should be soft, mellow, and diffused. Stay away from primary colors, pure colors, or colors with high chroma (brightness or intensity). You want to have a spark of color to create interest, but it shouldn't be so intense or overused that it ruins (or poisons) the rug by controlling it. An odd or

unusual use of color adds interest to a design and definitely makes it unique. Also, use colors with a variety of values (lightness or darkness). If all the colors are the same value, there will be a lack of contrast between the items of the design. Using several values of the same color adds charm. Medium values age a rug quickly; I especially like to use them as the background. However, you must be willing to spend more time and effort working with the colors so you don't lose your design completely.

Note the photographs of the original *Ligonier Duo* and three recently hooked versions. Each one has its own personality and feel, not only because of the fabrics chosen but also because of the hooking direction. This is an excellent opportunity to compare materials and techniques and see what appeals to you about each one.

CHAPTER 2

Designs and Patterns

To create an antique-looking rug, you need to re-create the atmosphere of the antique rugs you admire. You will notice that antique designs have several elements in common and are beautiful because of their simplicity. The antique creation is not cluttered or crowded; it usually features only one main object or theme. Furthermore, there is a complete lack of respect for scale, balance, perspective, or proportion. Attention is not paid to intricate details but to the overall motif and design. Most important, the design usually contains a personal or individual touch from the artist.

Our ancestors took ideas from everyday life—their families, important dates or events, and pleasant memo-ries. Regional themes are also common, ranging from marine motifs to landscapes. Frequently the designs are more like folk art, consisting of symbols, people, animals, or birds, and contain a bit of a surprise. The borders may have unusual patterns, whether they are still recognizable or not. Antique rugs usually have a charming, original look. These designs were created by unassuming, down-to-earth women or their husbands. Their intention was to create utilitarian items that happened to be pretty, interesting, or important to them—not works of art.

The word *whimsical* is often used to describe antique rug designs. Rug makers often express their emotions in their designs, incorporating individual touches. When designing a rug, it's important to use your imagination; artistic ability

Olde Hearts, 31" x 16". Hooked by Barbara Carroll. This whimsical rug with two hearts also contains an unidentifiable shape in the center and two shrub like growths beside it. The border, from another old rug, is a great hit-and-miss style, with corner designs anchoring it. (Printed by Woolley Fox in the *Keeping the Past Alive* series.)

is not required. Even it it's not perfect, it will be successful because it comes from your heart and soul.

USING COMMERCIAL PATTERNS

In the late 1800s, Edward Frost was selling printed patterns along his peddler's route, so even back then, not all homemakers were designing their own rugs. Today, there are many wonderful commercial patterns and designs available that are perfect for creating an antique-looking rug. One of the best catalogs is Barbara Carroll's, the Woolley Fox, which includes her original designs and those by Warren Kimble, Carol Andres, Madgalena Briner, Barbara Carroll, Edyth O'Neil of Red Cape Cottage, and more. Some of my other favorites are Fredericksburg Rugs, Spruce Ridge Studio, and

Patsy B. Look at as many catalogs as you can. The perfect design may already exist.

You can buy a designer's pattern and then alter it to suit your taste (just don't claim it as your own design; it is still copyrighted by the designer). One simple way to personalize a pattern is to remove one item and replace it with something else that has significance to you, such as a name or a special date. If a commercial design has too much clutter, you can remove specific parts of it or simply remove some of the lines. For instance, if the pattern has a particularly fussy flower with lots of detail, you can make two petals into one by removing a line. You are, in effect, redrawing the flower to make it more primitive. (I believe that's why fine-point Sharpie permanent markers were invented—so we could make changes on commercial pat-

Santa with Deer, 34" x 28". Designed by Marian Ham, Quail Hill Designs. Hooked by Martha Reynolds of Dallas, Texas. Martha took this commercially designed rug and made it unique by giving both Santa and the deer wonderfully startled expressions. The plaid she used for the antlers is great— blue antlers! I particularly like her use of hit and miss in the cat-paw circles for the border.

Heart Kit, 12" x 15". Designed and hooked by P. D. Hankamer of Hankamer, Texas. This simple design was made great by the use of color. Also note the S shapes hooked in the background. Any beginner would be lucky to start hooking with this kit.

terns.) Even if you hook a preprinted pattern without altering the design, you can make it distinctive by using specific fabrics and colors.

If you purchase a preprinted pattern, check to make sure that it wasn't printed crooked. To do this, take a pencil and drag it in the holes following the outside perimeter on two sides of the pattern. Hold the pencil at a 45-degree angle—don't hold it straight up and down or flat. If the pattern has been printed correctly, your drawn pencil line will follow the pattern maker's line. If it doesn't, you have three options: (1) Hook the pattern as is, though this is not recommended. Hooking along a straight line on the perimeter of the rug will make finishing the edges much easier. (2) Use a different color Sharpie and correct the pattern. Sometimes this is very easy to do, and sometimes it's impossible to do. If it's a geometric pattern, don't even try to correct it. (3) Return the pattern to the designer and get a refund or ask for a pattern printed on the straight of the grain. This is the best option. You are investing a lot of time and money to create a family heirloom, and you deserve to have a perfectly drawn pattern.

Stars, Hearts, and Diamonds, 26" x 24". Designed and hooked by Cindy Trick of Beavercreek, Ohio. Cindy took several common, everyday items and made a great rug with them. Notice that two sides have lamb's tongue, while the other two do not. Hooking each of the hearts in the center a little differently gives the rug more interest. (Photographed by Larry Bosley, Encore Production Services, Cincinnati, Ohio.)

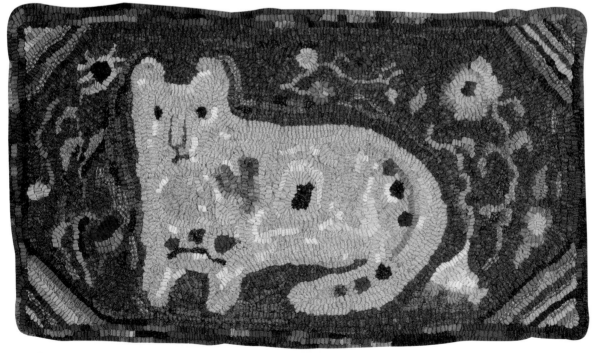

Garden Cat, 30" x 17". Designed and hooked by Pat Freasier of Houston, Texas. The face on this cat is marvelous. He gives the impression of being in control. I especially like the purple heart and the flowers on the cat's coat. The treatment Pat used on the corners was a smart move, as it serves to calm down the rug.

My Beloved, 29" x 33".
Designed by Jill Paterson.
Hooked by Pat Freasier of
Houston, Texas. Here, the
movement in the background
works well because the
design is so simple. I love the
fatness of the birds' legs.

Antique Flower Basket,
34" x 24". This photograph of
the edge of an antique rug
shows why we don't use
burlap for the backing. It also
shows one way of finishing
the edges that shouldn't be
used if you're going to place
the rug on the floor. (From
the author's collection.)

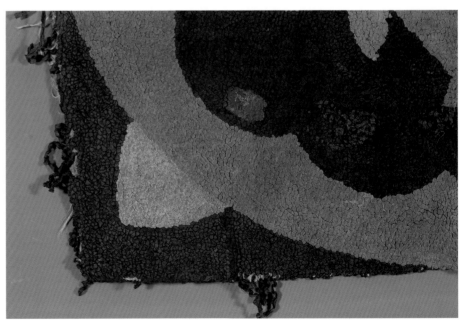

It is also possible to buy kits that contain a design and precut wool; you can then make simple changes in color or fabric to obtain a more antique-looking result. If you find a kit you like, don't hesitate to purchase it. You can easily make minor substitutions to customize it, and any leftover wool can always be used in another project. Rug hookers waste nothing.

DESIGNING YOUR OWN PATTERNS

If you decide to be more creative and draw your own design, it should reflect your personality and sense of style. Inspiration for a design can come from many places—everyday objects, life experiences, or other people. Ideas usually don't just spring into our heads (although I have awakened in the middle of the night with part of a rug designed), but they can be found all around us. If you don't feel confident enough to draw your own design, there are many other options. You can have an artistic friend draw a design for you. You can have your child, a neighbor's child, or your grandchild draw an animal or other object and then turn that drawing into a rug. In addition, numerous books are available with reprintable designs, subjects, and items. One of the most well-known series is by Dover Publications and can be purchased at most bookstores. Susan Quicksall of Texas has a wonderful booklet—*A Sampler of Historical Design Motifs for the Rug Hooker*. It is filled with primitive items that can be duplicated and enlarged. Many of my students have found this book helpful and fun to use. The Association of Traditional Hooking Artists (ATHA) newsletter and *Rug Hooking* magazine sometimes offer free patterns. Most of these are for per-

King Arthur, 32" x 26". Hooked by Mary Magnuson of Stillwater, Minnesota, with $1/2$-inch-wide strips on linen. He definitely is the king, with even the whimsical stump paying tribute by standing at attention. Of particular interest are the spots of gold worked in the ground. Note the dark outline around his mane—it's not needed, but it looks great. (Printed by Woolley Fox in the *Keeping the Past Alive* series.)

sonal use and are not for commercial reproduction or sale.

When designing your own pattern, you may find it helpful to cut out paper templates and place them on the backing of your choice. This simple step takes the idea from your brain and turns it into something you can see. It allows you to determine whether the design works. Does something need to be eliminated or changed? Does part of the design need to be enlarged? Does the design fit well in the size you have chosen, or are adjustments necessary? But don't get hung up

worrying about proportion or balance. Remember, most old-time rug hookers weren't artists, and they weren't concerned about such things. They simply hooked the things they loved.

CHOOSING A BACKING OR FOUNDATION

Many of the antique rugs we come across today were hooked on burlap, which became easily accessible after the 1850s. Although there are currently many types of backings on the market, the three that work best with wide strips of wool are

Stars, Stars, Stars, 44" x 23". Designed and hooked by Judy Soehnge of Yoakum, Texas. The stars are floating on a dark but aged background. The unusual shape of the border works because of the wonderful colors. Judy repeats some of the colors throughout the rug, but not all of them. By using the colors in varying amounts, she keeps the eye moving. But the greatest thing about this rug is the unexpected use of the squares in each corner. As this rug ages, it will become a great antique-looking rug.

primitive linen, monk's cloth, and primitive burlap. I prefer linen, but many rug hookers love working with the softer and evenly spaced monk's cloth, which is made from cotton. I don't recommend using burlap. Even though today's burlap is much better than what our ancestors used, it deteriorates much faster than either linen or monk's cloth (see the accompanying photograph on page 12 showing what happens to burlap foundations). Do you really want to spend all that time designing, planning, and hooking a rug only to have it begin to fall

apart in fifty years or sooner? You may not be around that long, but remember that you are making an antique for the future, so why not use the best material available for your base? I suggest that you try hooking on both linen and monk's cloth and see which one you prefer.

If you're buying a commercial pattern, most designers will put the pattern on the backing of your choice. There may be an extra charge, but I think it's well worth it. I also prefer that commercial patterns be printed on the straight of the grain. Not everyone feels that way, but it makes it much easier to hook any straight lines—leaving you a nice straight edge to finish—and the completed rug will lay better on the floor.

If you're transferring your own design (see below), cut the foundation larger than the pattern. My preference is to have 5 inches around the perimeter of the design. For example, if my finished pattern is 25" x 35", I cut the linen backing to measure 35" x 45". You can get by with less clearance around the pattern, and many find 5 inches to be wasteful. But I like the option of easily making the pattern larger, and I don't have to struggle to keep the rug on the frame when working on the outside borders.

You also need to stabilize the edges of the foundation to prevent fraying or raveling. The most common way is to serge the edges or to zigzag two rows of stitching around the edges. If you don't have access to a sewing machine, don't worry. Another option is to use masking tape. If the masking tape is narrow, place it around the edges on both sides of the foundation. If the tape is wide, you can place it on one side and then fold it over so it covers the back side of the foundation.

If I'm transferring my own design, I perform one more step: find the center of the precut piece of backing. The simplest way to do this is to fold the backing into fourths. The corner that has no edge showing is the center. Mark that point with a Sharpie. When you open the foundation, there should be a mark in the center. Then do the same with the pattern. Aligning the two center marks ensures that there are equal amounts of backing on all sides.

TRANSFERRING YOUR OWN DESIGNS

Several options are available for transferring a design to the backing. One of the easiest is to make paper templates, place them in the correct position, and trace them with a Sharpie. I prefer to use black initially so that my changes can be made in other colors. You can also use Red Dot Tracer (similar to interfacing, but with equally spaced red dots to help with alignment), nylon organdy (also known as bridal netting), or window screening. I prefer the Red Dot Tracer method; however, if numerous copies will be made of a pattern, screening works better because the traced lines don't bleed or increase in width as much. Personally, I find nylon netting difficult to work with. My suggestion is to start with Red Dot Tracer and if you don't like it, try the other methods.

Follow these step-by-step directions for transferring your own design:

- Draw your design on paper.
- Place Red Dot Tracer on top of the paper design, taking care to align the red dots with any straight lines in your pattern.
- Place weights on or pin down the Red Dot Tracer.
- Trace the design using a pen or extra-fine-point Sharpie.
- Lift the Red Dot Tracer off the paper, and voila! You have your pattern.
- Next, you need to prepare your chosen backing, which should be several inches larger than the pattern. First, you need to find the straight of the grain. The easiest way to do this is to take a pencil, place it in one of the openings of the fabric, and pull it toward your body at an angle. The pencil should be at about a 45-degree angle; don't hold the pencil straight up and down, and don't hold it parallel to the foundation. The pencil will easily glide in a straight line, leaving a visible line showing the straight of the grain. Repeat this action in both directions—the width and length of the backing.

Then follow these steps:

- Carefully place the Red Dot Tracer pattern on the foundation, taking the time to align the red dots along the straight of the grain. (Alternatively, you can mark the outside borders on the foundation first.)
- Place weights on or pin down the pattern to keep it in place.

- Slowly trace the pattern onto the backing using a Sharpie. The ink will soak through the tracer onto the backing. If you start in the middle, you should get less ink on your hands, but it can be easily removed with rubbing alcohol.
- Remove the weights and Red Dot Tracer. Your pattern should be completely visible. If not, retrace as necessary (using a brand-new Sharpie should eliminate the need to retrace).
- Another easy but less common way to transfer a design involves the use of a light box, which is basically a box with a glass top that has a light bulb inside. You put the paper pattern directly on top of the glass, place the foundation on top of the pattern, turn on the light, and start tracing. You can either buy a light box or make one yourself. For years, I used my 42-inch-square, glass-topped breakfast table as an impromptu light box, which made transferring my own designs very easy. All I had to do was put a lamp (minus the shade) under the table to create a great light box. So check your household to see whether you might have a light box lurking somewhere.

COPYRIGHT

I would be remiss if I didn't mention copyright law. Patterns are copyrighted, which means that the artist has the exclusive right to the artistic work regardless of whether he or she decides to sell, copy, or distribute it. Copyright protection also allows the artist to make income from the creation. Familiar objects such as a star can't be copyrighted; however, an arrangement or design using stars can be copyrighted. If you use a pattern that says "designed by" someone, you should assume that it is copyrighted. In simple terms, if you copy a copyrighted pattern without paying for it, you are stealing. It is the same as if you took money directly from the designer's pocket.

I know of several people who have received "cease and desist" orders, and more than one has actually been sued in court and lost. You are on much safer ground if you buy a commercial pattern (and make changes if you like, but don't claim it as your own) or design your own pattern from scratch. Even if you copy an antique rug that no longer has copyright protection, it is best to identify it as an antique rug on your label. It's only fair to give the original designer some credit.

There is one instance when you can legally copy a copyrighted design: if the designer has published the pattern (such as in a book) and given you permission to make a copy for your personal use. Examples are Pat Cross's *Purely Primitive* and Barb Carroll's *Antique Folk Art Rug Hooking*. This release is only for your personal use, however; you can't make these patterns and sell them. Play by the rules, and you will be fine.

MISCONCEPTIONS ABOUT COPYRIGHTS

- "It's okay to make copies after I buy the first printed pattern." **Not true.** You can't buy a pattern, make copies, and give them to your friends.
- "It's okay to make a second copy of the pattern for my own use." **Not true.** It's like buying a coat: if you buy a coat that you like, you can't simply walk into the store and take another one without paying.
- "If I change a specific percentage of the pattern, it's okay to reuse the pattern or call it my own." **Not true.** Even if you change 50 percent of the pattern, the original artist may still claim copyright infringement.
- "It's okay because I'm only making a rug for my personal use." **Not true.** If the rug is *ever* exhibited or photographed, legal problems may ensue. The rug won't disappear when you leave this earth, and the next owner might not be willing to keep it in a closet at home.

CHAPTER 3

Color

If you were given an assortment of rug photographs and asked to pick out your favorites, your choices would likely be based on the colors used, not the design. Color is the lure that draws you to a particular rug. Your eye first recognizes color and color arrangement; the design is secondary. The best learning tool to help you become comfortable using color is your intuition. Look at art books, magazines, and other people's rugs and decide what you like and don't like about each one. This is good practice for color planning.

If you want to be scientific about color planning, there are many wonderful books to guide you, including *The Enjoyment and Use of Color* by Walter Sargent and *Color* by Faber Birren. When I first started hooking rugs, I bought every book on color I could find, but that's not really necessary. Anyone can color plan; it may be a little harder for some, but it's within everyone's grasp. Think about getting dressed for a special occasion: you know which shoes look best with a particular outfit, don't you? Think about children coloring with crayons before they've had any instruction: they don't care about spe-

Dog, 30" x 22". Hooked by Barbara Daniels of Sugar Land, Texas. This rug illustrates great use of colors in the background, with an interesting fabric employed to outline the dog, but most fun is the whitish area under the dog. (Printed by Woolley Fox in the *Keeping the Past Alive* series.)

Tulip Cross, 48" x 48". Hooked by Katie Hartner of Tyler, Texas, with a #8 cut on linen. Great colors make a beautiful rug. Here, all the different greens used in the leaves give them life, but the crowning touch is outlining the gold flowers in the main motif with red. (Printed by Emma Lou Lais.)

cific colors or color placement—they're just having fun. That's the feeling I'd like you to experience.

Two or three colors plus a background color make the simplest color plan for a rug. You know which colors you like, but also study the environment in your home. Your decorating colors can be very different from the colors you like or the colors you wear. Although it's not neces-

BASIC TERMS RELATED TO COLOR

Color or hue: the name given to a color, such as blue.
Value: the lightness or darkness of a color.
Chroma: the intensity, brightness, or strength of a color.
Complements: colors directly opposite each other on the color wheel.
Contrast: the amount of difference between two elements, such as value or color.

Olde Cats, 35" x 26". This grand antique rug is one of the oldest I have seen. It was created with a mixture of fabrics. It looks like the rug hooker drew her own cats in the center but then "borrowed" the border, perhaps from a neighbor's pattern. This sharing among friends is part of our rug hooking history that needs to be acknowledged. I particularly love how the reds are used in the top portion of the border. (From the collection of Dorothy Panaceck of Fredericksburg, Texas. Printed by Stonehill Spinning.)

sary to know where the finished rug will go, if you've already made the decision, it will be easier to pick out the colors.

COLOR THEORY

Color theory involves the concept of how colors work with one another. Listed below are some basic tenets of color theory applicable to rug hooking (for those who need such guidelines):

- Use a color only once to draw attention to that area.
- Repeat colors, even if they're not the same value or intensity.
- Balance the use of colors—triangular balance, or use 3, 5, or 7 (the practice of using odd rather than even numbers, which is the same method florists use when arranging flowers).
- Colors that are being balanced need not be the same value—they can be lighter or darker.
- Dark colors make objects look smaller.

- Don't use black for outlining. Use dark blue, gray, or even purple instead.
- Neutrals, particularly grays, let the eye rest.
- Use light, dark, bright, and dull in your rug, but not in equal amounts.
- Carry colors from the central motif to the border.
- Choose your background first, because that determines the look of your rug—light and airy or dark and heavy.
- One part of the rug—a central motif, a border, or the background—should dominate. The other parts should support the main element.
- Dark and dull colors tend to be distant.
- Light items placed on dark backgrounds tend to more forward.
- Light colors tend to have less visual weight than dark colors.
- Warm colors (think reds) tend to come forward, while cool colors (think blues) tend to retreat.

Standing Deer, 26" x 26". Designed by Laurice Heath of Fredericksburg, Texas. Hooked by Cynthia Norwood with #8 and #9 cuts on linen. Basically, the motifs are one color family, with lots of antique paisley, and the background is another color family. The deer has a thin halo to give him a little more importance. In the close-up, take note of the fake repairs on the right side. It's easy to imagine that this piece was damaged and then "fixed."

- Warm colors are more exciting; they attract your eye and grab your attention.
- Cool colors are more relaxing and slow down action.
- Use color combinations that exist in the real world.
- The smaller the area, the brighter the color can be.

COLOR PLANNING FOR AN ANTIQUE LOOK

Keep in mind that we're interested in hooking a rug that has an antique look. Therefore, many of the rules that apply to traditional rug hooking are not important. Although we're trying to duplicate the subdued look of an antique rug, it's important to understand that the antique rugs we love didn't start out with that soft, muted look. The original colors were vibrant and full of life—as you can tell if you look at the reverse side of an old rug.

Several factors helped these rugs achieve their wonderful mellow color combinations: wear, exposure to light, original dye, and time. Most of these antique rugs were not considered works of art when they were created; rather, they were utilitarian objects placed on the floor for the comfort of the family. Their beauty was an added benefit. Everyday wear introduced dust and dirt to the wool fibers, and exposure to light caused the colors to fade.

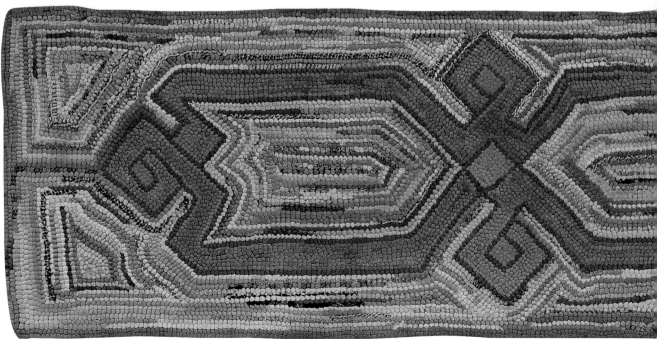

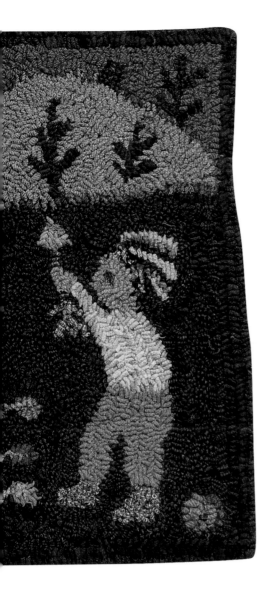

Brave Hunter, 40;" x 20". Hooked by Barbara Carroll. This is a wonderful nonsensical rug with great colors. Where will the arrow land? Take note of the purple flower and the colors of the feathers in his headdress. (Printed by Woolley Fox in the *Keeping the Past Alive* series.)

All colors fade when exposed to sunlight, but blue is particularly susceptible; the reds seem to be the least affected. Old-fashioned dyes and dyeing methods were less colorfast compared with current techniques. And of course, the one thing that ages everything is time.

It is imperative to understand that rug hookers of the past couldn't run to the store to buy a specific color wool. They used what was on hand, even if it wasn't the perfect color. If they ran out of one kind of wool, they substituted whatever was available and kept on hooking. Since it's difficult for us to duplicate that situation, it's okay to plan ahead. Pick out the wools for your project, then add one small piece that's definitely off-color—either much lighter or darker than the rest. Decide exactly where you want to hook that unusual piece to give the effect of running out of wool; it's easiest to do this in the background. The same technique can be used to re-create fake patches or stains on your rug. Use a color

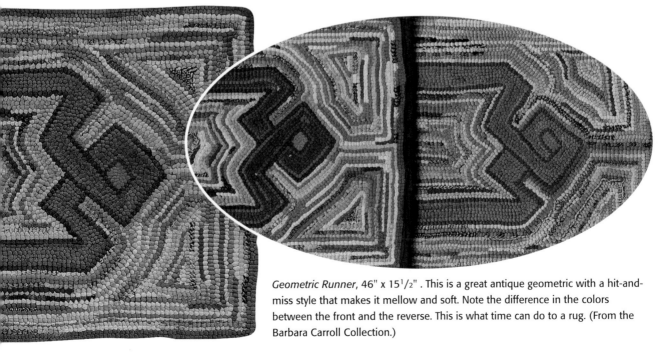

Geometric Runner, 46" x 15^1/$_2$" . This is a great antique geometric with a hit-and-miss style that makes it mellow and soft. Note the difference in the colors between the front and the reverse. This is what time can do to a rug. (From the Barbara Carroll Collection.)

Deer and Oak Leaves,
57" x 30". Designed by Joan Moshimer. Hooked by Jenny Rupp of West Chester, Ohio, with a #8 cut on linen. This is already a very old looking rug that will get even better with time. Special features include the white antlers, the bed of lamb's tongue the deer is resting in, and the softness of the scrolls and acorns. (Photographed by Larry Bosley, Encore Production Services, Cincinnati, Ohio.)

that's in the same family but different enough to be noticeable.

Also predominant in antique rugs is the unusual or unexpected use of colors. Unfortunately, we don't know whether this was planned or whether these rug hookers just ran out of a certain fabric and substituted something else. I prefer to believe that by adding an unexpected color they were expressing their own personalities. Thus, you might see cats with red whiskers or roosters with green combs, which is something you can easily imitate. Look at your pattern before you start to hook and decide where it would be fun and interesting to add an unusual color. Frequently, reds, purples, and teals are chosen, but use your own color sense. We all have in our stashes pieces of unusual wool that we wonder why we bought or

how we will ever use, and this is the perfect place to incorporate those pieces.

When most people think of primitive antique rugs, browns and grays come to mind. These neutral colors predominate because blues often fade into grays and greens may become browns. To replicate that look, pick blues that lean toward a softer or grayish hue, greens that are not full of vim and vigor, and reds that lean toward a rusty red or peachy orange. These colors aren't dark or dreary but rather muted by the fading process. If any of the fabrics that you've chosen are too bright, they can be toned down (see chapter 9 on dyeing techniques). But you must be careful not to tone them down so much that you end up with a flat, dull rug that looks like it was made 200 years ago and used to patch a roadway. You still want color and a

not be pleasing to the eye, and you could lose the design. Some rug hookers don't like to use textured wool because it's difficult to envision the final result—different textures yield different results. You can try rolling a textured piece of fabric tightly to gauge the expected result, or try scrunching the fabric into accordion folds to approximate how it will hook. The best method, however, is to actually cut and hook a strip to see how it looks, giving you a better idea of how it will relate to different colors and other pieces of fabric.

Become more familiar with the use of textures by picking up pieces of fabric and imagining what they could be used for and how they might hook; then actually test them. When you look at these textured pieces, what colors do you recognize? With practice, you will learn what textures can do. For example, textures with similar colors in similar values can easily be blended to make an area more interesting, but not shocking. Using textures with different values of the same color adds interest to a rug. Specific design features lend themselves to certain textures: for rocks and stones, gray and brown herringbones are perfect; light and dark gray herringbones make great mortar; various green plaids give trees depth and interest, without you even thinking about it; small, neutral, patterned textures are soft and give the eye a place to rest.

When I first started using textures, I cut a square piece of the fabric and stapled it to a piece of linen. Next to that piece of fabric, I hooked a square so that I had a sample of how it would look when hooked. Although this is time-consuming, it may pay off in the long run when color planning a rug. Experience is the best teacher. We are lucky to have such an extensive variety of ready-to-hook textures available. Just a few years back, the supply was so limited that overdyeing was often a necessity. Most of my rugs are now made with "as-is" wools—that is, wools that have not been overdyed but simply washed. I prefer to avoid commercially dyed solid fabrics, but if you must use

variety of values in the rug. When I'm planning a rug, I like to place all my fabrics on the floor at the bottom of the stairs, where I pass by several times a day. Each time I do, my eye automatically takes in how well the wools work together (or not), and it registers in my brain—where all important color decisions are made.

One of the easiest ways to get an antique look is to use plaids, tweeds, heathers, checks, and other textured wools. These fabrics have color, but because of the weaving process, it is usually muted, producing a softer and warmer rug. When using textured fabrics, choose an assortment of patterns—that is, textures and plaids of different sizes or patterns. For instance, if you were to use the same size plaid in different colors throughout the rug, the effect might

Sample of how textured wools look when hooked. This is a great exercise if you've never used textured fabrics.

them, overdye them with their complement to soften the color.

The background color dictates the overall look of the rug, so color planning is easier if you decide up front whether you want the background to be light or dark. For an antique appearance, the best background is one made up of several similarly colored fabrics rather than just one fabric. Neutrals or grayed colors are excellent choices for the background. Many antique rugs use light backgrounds in the tan or camel family; darker backgrounds are usually brown, blue, or burgundy. Don't be afraid to choose a dark blue background and then mix in a few strips of wool that are dark teal, purple, or even black. These little spurts of color make the background not only more interesting but also more fun to hook. Medium-value backgrounds immediately age a rug, but some people find these values difficult to work with, because it may be necessary to outline or change the fabric at the edge of the design.

After choosing the background color, next you must pick three more colors for the rug. One color should be dominant—used more than the other two. These colors should look good together and have some contrast with the background. Place the three colors on the background color, and see whether the result is pleasing. If it

is, you're ready for the next step: determining the placement of the colors.

For color placement, there are basic rules that we normally follow, such as creating balance by repeating one color in several areas or using a plaid that has some of the dominant color in it. Frequently we use the 3, 5, 7 method of balancing colors, in the same way that floral arrangements are made. But remember, you are creating a primitive, antique-looking rug, and these rules were made to be broken. Keep in mind, however, that if changes in value occur too abruptly, and if they contrast too much, the rug won't be as attractive. Changes in value need to be slow and steady. Normally, the highest contrast is between the design and the background. You can hook a line to contain the design, but this line should be a textured fabric rather than a solid one; a solid fabric would create too sharp a line. Stay away from strong or bright colors. Any very bright color should be used sparingly—it is considered the spark (or, if overused, the poison). You don't want it to overwhelm the rug but rather create a spot of interest. To make the rug even more interesting, use textures in different values of a similar color. Take one fabric and scatter it throughout different areas of the rug. You don't need to hook an entire element with one color; perhaps

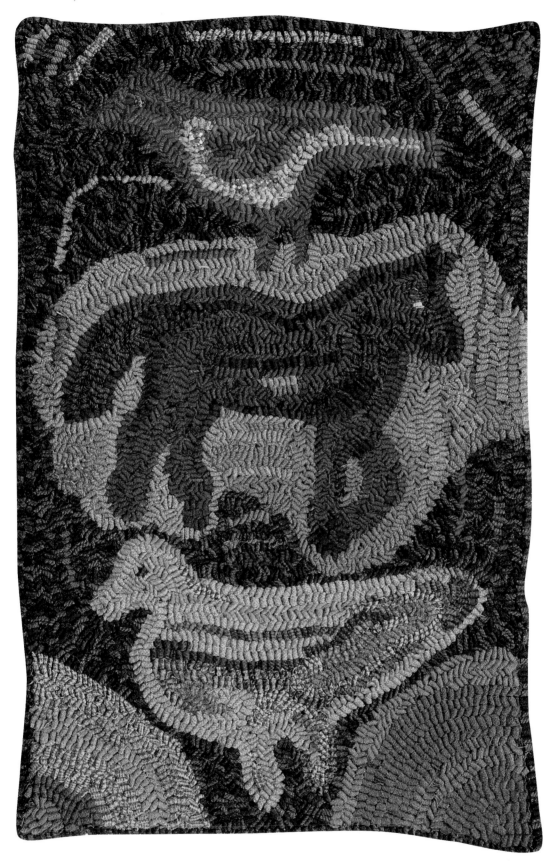

Harvey Magdalena, 23" x 34". Hooked by Mary Magnuson of Stillwater, Minnesota, with $^1/_2$-inch strips on linen. First of all, I love the purple in the two bottom corners. The halo around the horse is special because it keeps him from falling completely into the background. Old rugs often have highlights or halos around objects of importance. (Printed by Woolley Fox in the *Keeping the Past Alive* series.)

Floral Hall Runner, 3' x 20'. Designed and hooked by Judy Soehnge of Yoakum, Texas, with a #8 cut and hand-cut paisley. Just imagine the color journey Judy was on as she planned and hooked this rug. This beautiful rug will be enjoyed for years and will be a valued antique someday. She used lots of color, but it's soft color. The background of the outer border has a wonderfully aged look. (Photograph by Bobby, Stonehill Spinning)

GUIDELINES (NOT RULES) FOR PRIMITIVE RUG COLOR PLANNING

- Choose colors you like first.
- Avoid using two high-chroma colors next to each other.
- Heathers and tweeds age the rug immediately.
- Feel free to use a specific color only once.
- Outline with whatever color gives the desired effect.
- Don't worry about balancing using the rule of threes.
- Use color to create a sense of movement.
- Use bizarre or unconventional colors where they are least expected.
- Use bright colors—bright pink, purple, orange, or lime green—sparingly.
- Use both dyed and as-is wools.
- Highly contrasting values normally don't work well in backgrounds.
- Golds add warmth to a rug; neutrals tone it down.
- Pick a plaid for the border, and match the colors for use in your motif.

use it only as an outline or a shadow here and there. Then use the other two colors to carry the dominant color. Hook a row of background around your design as you go. That way, you can see how well it works and whether you need to make the background lighter or darker to get the result you want.

Think of color planning as a journey that includes both planned and unplanned stops, with some more exciting than others. All you need is a place to begin and a general idea of your destination. And give yourself the option to change that destination—you're working with wool and colors, after all, not a chisel and stone. The willingness to make changes may create a masterpiece. Let the rug speak to you as you hook it. Your goal is to create an arrangement of color that pleases you. Color is magic, and you are the magician. For more information on detailed color planning, see *Secrets of Color Planning in Hand Hooked Rugs* by Betty Krull.

CHAPTER 4

Width of Cuts and Hook Sizes

A ntique rugs were made with hand-cut strips of wool or other fabrics or with strips created by the cut-and-tear method. When inspecting antique rugs, it is obvious that the strips of wool are not of an equal width; this randomness simply adds to the rug's charm and interest. Also obvious: the strips are fairly wide—usually approximating a #8 ($^1/_4$") cutter head size or larger. To achieve the best results, you should mix your cuts. For example, if you use mainly #8, randomly mix in some #9 ($^3/_8$") or larger (#10 equals $^1/_2$"), or even some hand-cut strips of wool. Novice rug hookers or first-time primitive rug hookers may be more comfortable using a #8-cut; more experienced primitive rug hookers might use #10-cut strips or wider. Anything narrower than #8-cut doesn't do the primitive look justice, but these narrow strips may be used in small, random spots. Wide strips age the rug immediately because the colors are diffused by the textures in the wool fabric. The wider the strip of wool, the more you can see the pattern or texture of the fabric.

Primitive Basket, 36" x 24". Designed and hooked by Laurice Heath of Fredericksburg, Texas. The wool strips in the rug were all hand torn, and many pieces of recycled wool were used. Note the effective use of darker wool in the background to duplicate a stain. This is a soft, old-looking primitive with a wonderful basket. (Copyright Fredericksburg Rugs. Photographed by Layne Heath.)

Diamond Geometric, 36" x 36". An antique adaptation designed and hooked by Sally Kallin of Pine Island, Minnesota. By using great color play and #7, #8, and #9 cuts, Sally created a fun and fanciful rug. She also used some wonderful pieces of paisley that give this geometric more life. It will age well.

CUTTING YOUR WOOL

Hand-cut wool strips are cut one at a time with scissors. First, you have to remove the selvedge. Cut a snip parallel with the selvedge, and then tear it away from the rest of the yardage. Your wool strips will be the strongest if you cut them parallel to or in the same direction as the selvedge. Tear a fresh edge every few inches or so to make sure you stay on the straight of the grain. Any pair of scissors will do, but to make the job a little easier and faster, use a pair of spring-loaded scissors with an easy grip-handle (Fiskars is

the brand I use). Although this method is slow, many rug hookers feel a great sense of accomplishment when they hand-cut their strips. I hand- cut my strips only if I need just a small amount, my cutter has the wrong blade or cartridge, or I'm using an unusual fabric that needs a little extra attention when cutting.

The cut-and-tear method is one step quicker than the hand-cut approach (and I find it more relaxing). For instance, if you want to work with $1/2$-inch-wide strips, cut a snip in your wool at the 1-inch mark; tear that strip away from

Rose Oval,
23" x 46". The reds
certainly dominate, with
combinations of rusts, reds,
and pinks. But what makes this
old rug so charming is that the green
leaves stand back and let the roses be front
and center. (From the Barbara Carroll Collection.)

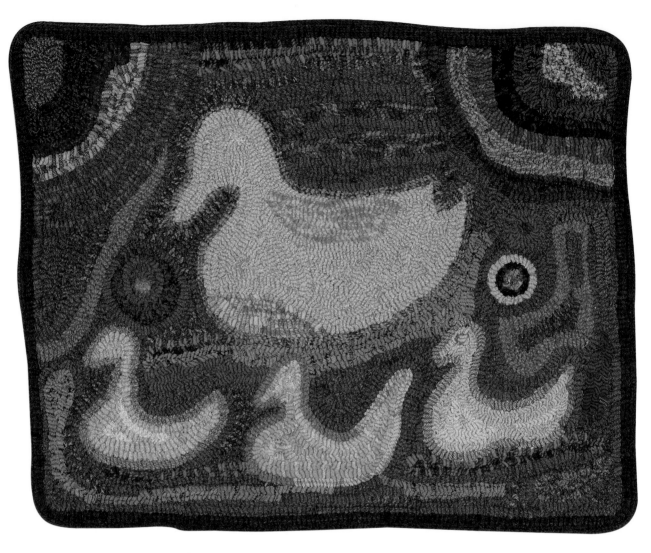

Olde Ducks, 30" x 25". Hooked by Barbara Daniels of Sugar Land, Texas. The bright blue lifts the rug and almost gives movement to the ducks. It also creates a wonderful unexpected area. (Pattern by Magdalena. Printed by Woolley Fox in the *Keeping the Past Alive* series.)

the rest of the yardage; and cut the strip of wool in half lengthwise—leaving you with two $^1/_2$-inch strips. The rough edges impart a unique look to your rug, but you'll have one edge that is on the straight of the grain—the torn edge. These wide strips allow more of the pattern and texture of the wool to show through. Depending on the weave of the wool, you may be able to tear narrower strips, such as $^1/_2$-inch strips that can be cut into two $^1/_4$-inch strips. Don't take the time to measure carefully; you don't want all the strips to be identical. The cut edges don't have to be perfect either. In fact, the imperfection only adds character to your rug.

You can also use strips that are completely torn by hand—no cutting involved. Many rug hookers love the more primitive look that results. Simply make a snip at the appropriate width, and

then tear. This technique works better with some wools than others; certain wools do not tear easily.

One method that I don't use at all is the rotary cutter. This tool has been most beneficial to the quilting world, but some rug hookers use it and like it. This method is much faster than cutting and tearing and less expensive than buying a mechanical cutter. It is imperative, however, that you cut on the straight of the grain and cut only one layer of fabric at a time. To determine whether your strips are on the straight of the grain, grasp the ends of a strip between the thumb and index finger of each hand; then give the strip a pulling or snapping motion. If this action results in fibers pointing away from the strip of wool, you are off the straight of the grain. Strips cut off the straight of the grain not only are weak but also may be impossible to hook with. To find the

straight of the grain again, simply make a snip at the top of the fabric and create a freshly torn edge to follow.

A mechanical cutter is the best choice if you want to make the task even faster and easier. There are many brands on the market; Rigby, Fraser, Bliss, and Townsend are the most well known. Each cutter has advantages and disadvantages, and each type has its own loyal following. Take advantage of every opportunity to try cutters different from your own, and ask the owners what they like about their machines. Although I have used and owned all the brands listed, my favorite is the Townsend. The blades are easy to change, and it has a very smooth, rhythmic cutting action. The disadvantage is that you need a table edge or a stand to clamp it to. Townsend sells a metal stand, but I use a collapsible wooden stand made by Cabin Crafts of Chardon, Ohio.

The Bliss cutter (by Harry M. Fraser Company) is a good choice for beginners because it is the least expensive and can be used on any flat surface.

When using a mechanical cutter, you first need to tear a strip of fabric to find the straight of the grain. It's best to work with a piece of wool that is 5 inches wide or less; the length is up to you. Always make your strips at least 15 inches long, however, to avoid too many starts and stops. I often use strips 24 inches long, especially when hooking background. The more experienced you are, the longer your strips are likely to be. Place the freshly torn edge against the guide or straightedge of the cutter. As you turn the handle, the fabric moves past the cutting wheel. Allow your non-turning hand to rest lightly on the wool just to hold it in place—don't push or pull. When you've finished making the first cut, take

Blummer Fraktur, 23" x 17". Hooked by Pam Fogle of Frisco, Texas. As these blues fade over time, this rug will become as soft as the antiques we value today.

the piece of fabric and flip it end to end, so that the last end out is now the first end to be cut. If you keep cutting the same piece in the same direction, you're likely to get off the straight of the grain. Stop cutting every so often and test your strips to see if you're still on the straight of the grain (as described earlier). If you're severely off the straight of the grain, the wool strip it may actually break in half when you snap it. If so, make a fresh tear and continue cutting. I prefer to keep my strips in orderly bundles, tied with one strip of wool. Some rug hookers put different colors in different plastic bags (okay for short periods, but not for storage); others simply cut the strips and mix them all together in a basket.

CHOOSING A HOOK

The choice of a hook is a personal one. It is important to find one or two that feel comfortable for the way you hook. I use several: Nancy Miller pencil primitive hook, Nancy Miller Coco Bola coarse hook, Nancy Miller Clover hook, and Hartman ergo long handle. Because I'm one of those rug hookers who holds the hook like a pencil, the longer hooks work best for me. If you "palm" the hook—that is, hold it mainly in the palm of your hand—you might like the Hartman ball hook or the Richie hook. Most beginners start off with the inexpensive Moshimer hook, but whichever hook you choose, make sure it has a large or thick shank for primitives. By making a larger hole, this shank allows you to pull the wide strips through the foundation more easily. If you hook more than a couple of hours at a time, I strongly recommend that you switch hooks for a while. This allows your muscles to rest and lessens the chance of repetitive injury.

Unlike our ancestors, who had to make do with bent nails or other hand-made tools, we can buy a good utilitarian hook for about $5 or a beautiful, exotic wood hook for $50 or more. Using the best tools makes the job even more enjoyable. If you hook with a group, don't be shy about asking to try another member's hook. Most rug hookers will be pleased to tell you why they like a specific hook. Take the time to find the hook that is right for you, regardless of the look or the cost. This is a one-time purchase if you keep it in a safe place.

CHAPTER 5

Hooking the Main Design

To achieve the look of an antique rug, you need to give yourself permission to break the rules and have fun. Of course, there are some basic guidelines that should be followed. One of my main rules is not to cross or carry over the hooking strips on the back of the rug. Crossing over not only makes for a lumpy rug but also accelerates the wear in those areas. Instead of cross-

ing over, simply pull the strip up, cut it, and then start hooking in another area. The reverse side of the rug should be smooth and free of twisted wool, lumps, bumps, or crossovers. Take the time to actually look at the back of the rug or run your hand across it as you're hooking to make sure that it's nice and smooth.

When I'm ready to start hooking, I tend to gravitate directly to my favorite color and hook the motif that uses

Magdalena's Dogs and Cats, 38" x 31". Hooked by Mary Magnuson with ¹/₂-inch strips of wool. Note that the cat on the left is highlighted, perhaps signifying that this one was a favorite. The cat in the top right corner is hooked mainly in one color value, which works because it is so small. If Mary had hooked the dog using the same technique, the rug would not be as appealing. In the close-up of the dog, notice the direction of the hooking—some sections follow the contour, while others don't.

that color first, regardless of where it is in the pattern. Some rug hookers prefer to start hooking in the center and hook outward. It's generally easiest to start with the motif that's closest to the "surface." For example, if your pattern is a scene of a house with a tree in front of it, hook the tree before you hook the house. Outline the motif first and then fill it with your choice of fabrics, mixing textures and colors. The rug would be boring if every leaf were hooked in identical colors or fabrics. You may choose to make many of them

the same or similar, but feel free to make some of them radically different. Even throwing in a completely unexpected color is acceptable. It's best to hook directly on the line or a little inside the outline of the motif to keep your design from expanding too much. The use of wide strips of wool causes the design to appear larger until you hook a row of background fabric around it to define it or lock it in place.

We often hook a particular item by following its natural contours, but if you

Old Nutfield, 31" x 63". Designed by Ruth Hall. Hooked by Cindy Trick of Beavercreek, Ohio. Note the unusual directional hooking of the red flower. (Photographed by Larry Bosley, Encore Production Services, Cincinnati, Ohio.)

Magdalena's Bed Rug, 7' x 9'. Hooked by Kathy Applegate of Fort Worth, Texas. This rug took six months to complete. An entire chapter could be written about the hooking styles and colors used in this exquisite rug. Note how some of the animals are hooked with only one fabric and by following the contour of the animal. This provides a space to rest your eye. Look at the green duck at the top right—the wavy lines in the body make you think of a duck floating on a pond. The way the horse on the right is hooked makes it seem like he is never still. But my favorite is the dog on the left—the dog is outlined, but his body is hooked in straight lines. (Printed by Woolley Fox in the *Keeping the Past Alive* series.)

take the time to study antique rugs, you'll notice that this wasn't always done. For example, you may see an apple hooked as if it had been colored by a first-grader, with strokes made directly across the apple rather than following the contour of the piece of fruit. Or the rug hooker may have abruptly changed fabrics in the middle of the apple. Perhaps some apples were hooked by following the contour, but one was hooked totally out of character. The direction of the hooking can be used to emphasize a motif's importance by drawing attention to it. Consequently, a change in the direction of the hooking can create more interest and give the rug a certain quirkiness. Allow yourself the freedom to ignore the contour of a particular element or motif. Lose your perfection complex! Try to tap into the freedom of a child who is just learning how to color. This gives the rug a whimsical, intriguing, and individual appearance, the hallmark of an antique rug.

CHAPTER 6

Hooking the Background

You will notice that I devote much more space to hooking the background than hooking the main design. For some reason, most people have no trouble hooking the main design once they have it color planned, but they agonize over what to do about the background.

There are two main elements of the background: color and hooking style. There are as many theories about background as there are rug hookers. Some are adamant that you must first choose a background color; others think that it's sufficient to decide on a light versus dark background and worry about the specific color after the motifs are finished. A third group, made up mainly of primitive rug hookers, prefers to let the rug tell them not only what colors and values to use but also how to actually hook the background.

Backgrounds are so important because they can make or break a rug. A wonderful motif can be lost in a background that's too busy. The background should be a bridesmaid—not the bride. The background is there to support and enhance the design, not overpower it. The choices you make in treating the background are vital—they can make the design pop, or they can make it fade and sink—so dealing with the background should not be an afterthought. Give your background as much consideration as you do the motif and borders, because it affects the entire rug.

Many factors influence your choice of background. Here are a few to consider:

- Do you want a light, airy rug or a heavy, dramatic rug? Do you want a silent background or one with movement?
- If you visualize movement, do you see a lot of movement or only a little?
- Do you want a quiet background that allows the design or motifs to dominate?
- How much background is in the rug?
- Is your pattern composed of mainly straight lines or curves?

Paisleys for Texas, 18" x 36". Designed and hooked by Cynthia Norwood with a #9 cut and hand-cut wool and paisley. The background is muddled and has an aged look. But if you look closely, you'll see that most of the design has a highlight around it. Fifteen different fabrics were used in the background. Because of the similarity of values used in the vase, many people don't notice the state of Texas at first glance.

Top, *Magdalena's Dog and Crows*, 42" x 34". Hooked in the original size by Lois Lee Ewing of Kerville, Texas, after she spotted the original in an auction catalog in 2000. Bottom, *Magdalena's Dog and Crows*, 30" x 23". Hooked by Pat Freasier of Houston, Texas. Both of these are great rugs, but note the difference in the backgrounds. Although I would consider both of these medium values, Lois chose a darker fabric than Pat's. Both backgrounds are full of movement and contain spots of color, but they allow the motifs to be grounded. Lois's is cut and tear, whereas Pat used #8 and #8.5 cuts. (Printed by Woolley Fox in the *Keeping the Past Alive* series.)

Early Basket, 48" x 30". Hooked by Cindy Hartman of Williamsburg, Virginia, with a #9-cut on linen. The pattern is based on an antique rug. This is a fabulous example of a medium-value background in a color that isn't used as background very often—blue. It works well because most of the motif is in gold and orange.

Early Basket, hooked by Cindy Hartman, illustrates echo hooking. It is easy to see the movement because of the different values of blue.

COLOR: LIGHT, MEDIUM, OR DARK?

Most people think that color is the most important factor, and for many, it is the most difficult decision. But even color choice can be simple when you're creat-ing an antique-looking rug. If you study antique rugs, you'll see that the back-ground is rarely a vivid color; most are done with neutral colors such as browns, grays, and blacks. For our ancestors, the decision was based on availability; they

probably looked at their piles of wool, realized that they had a lot of background to cover, and chose whatever color they had the most of.

For you, the first step is to decide whether you want a light, medium, or dark background. Working with a dark background is easiest for most rug hookers. A darker background tends to make the design "pop," and it creates a more dramatic and heavier rug. If the background is dark, you'll need to use medium to light values in the areas next to the background. Dark values on a dark background make a weak rug; the edges will be lost, and the motif will fade. If you decide to use a light background, you'll need to use medium to dark values around the edges of the motif where it makes contact with the background; otherwise, the motif will disappear. But because the goal is to create a rug that looks antique, don't worry if part of your motif fades away into the background.

If you have a large degree of contrast between the motif and the background, the design will be easily recognized, but the antique look will be compromised if you use sharp jumps of value—for exam-ple, a very light value next to a very dark background. This would never occur in a real antique rug because, over time, the light value would have become darker, and the dark value would have become lighter. Ideally, you want to avoid a high degree of contrast between background and motif, but create enough contrast to allow your eye to pause and enjoy the details. If you end up with an area where there isn't enough contrast to easily depict the motif, hook in part of a row of a quirky or unusual color to create the break you need.

The best background for an antique-looking rug is one that is made up of medium values—not light, not dark, but somewhere in between. Medium values can help you create a soft, subtle rug or a rug with an aged look. Neutral colors—gray, ecru, beige, tan, grunge green—are best for this technique. But if you're using a medium value for the background, you need to give some thought to the values used on the edges of the motif. If they are also medium, the motif may be completely lost and sink or fade into the background. For an antique-looking rug,

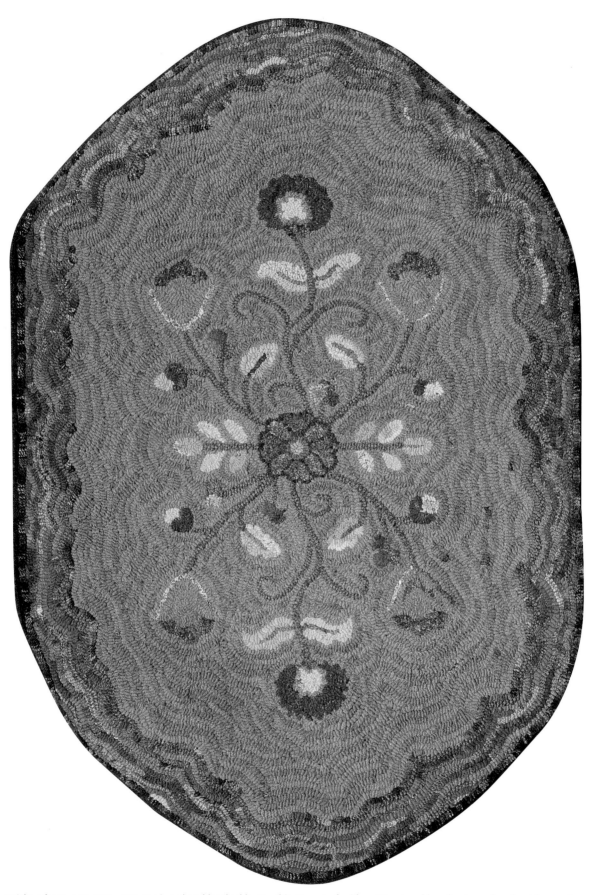

Paisleys for Guests, 36" x 52". Designed and hooked by Cynthia Norwood with a #9-cut and hand-cut wool and paisley on linen. The center almost gets lost, but it works because of the echo-hooked background in a medium value and the hit-and-miss border that duplicates colors in the motif. It ends up being a rug, which is perfect for a guest room. Note that leaves don't necessarily have to be green.

Seventeenth-Century Bed Rugg, 9' x 12'. Designed by Marion Ham of Quail Hill Designs. Hooked by Judy Soehnge of Victoria, Texas, with a #9-cut and hand-cut paisley. The lighter outside border keeps this rug from being heavy, and the narrow, dark outside edge keeps it from floating away. Judy hit the mark perfectly with this border treatment. (Photographed by Mercer Photography, Victoria, Texas.)

Magdalena's Folk Art Horse, 41" x 25". Hooked by Mary Magnuson with ¹/₂-inch strips on linen. This rug doesn't have an official border; it's framed by just two rows of hooking. The wonderful treatment of the two ends finishes the rug and directs your attention to the light horse on the light background. (Printed by Woolley Fox in the *Keeping the Past Alive* series.)

you don't want the design to really pop, but you don't want it to be lost either; it needs to be seen and easily recognized. The easiest way to accomplish this is by using darker or lighter values than the background on the edges of the motif. Alternatively, you can outline the entire motif or just a part of it with a contrasting color or value. Because of the real possibility of a lack of contrast, a medium-value background is the trickiest to do well. And of all the medium-value colors, gray is the hardest to use effectively. Grays often look too cold and dead and don't do justice to your rug. You can solve this problem by giving the gray fabric a dye wash with one of the warm colors you're using in the motif.

HOOKING STYLE

Once you've decided on a light, medium, or dark background and have chosen the color that looks best with your motif or design, you have another important decision to make: how are you going to hook the background? Once again, I suggest studying antique rugs. Although there are many styles of hooking that can be used for the background (see *Rug Hooking* magazine's June/July/August 2005 issue), there are only a few that work when trying to replicate the antique style. Echo hooking, halo effect, blocking, and random and S shapes are the ones most commonly used.

Echo

Echo hooking may be the easiest style, and it should be familiar to those of you who quilt. You hook one row of background around the motif, hook another row next to it, and then continue to follow the "echo" around each motif in the design until the background rows begin to meet. Echoing is also possible around a central design such as a spray of flowers. Eventually, you end up with small triangular or odd-shaped areas in the background that can just be filled in. Echoing is more interesting if you use several values of the same fabric or the same value of several different fabrics.

Halo

With halo hooking, the finished effect looks as if there is a halo surrounding the main motif. This technique is usually used when there is only one main motif that you want to draw attention to. To accomplish the halo effect, hook from one to several rows of a lighter background; then gradually move into a darker or medium value for the rest of the background.

Blocking

Blocking is used to separate the background into several different areas. These areas don't have to be identical, nor do they have to be squares or rectangles, although those are the most common shapes used. Each block is hooked in a different fabric, but the fabrics are usually similar in color or hue. This technique is used most effectively when the design consists of a very simple motif.

Random

To get the best effect from the random style, you need to use several different fabrics. These fabrics can be the same color with different values, or they can even be different colors if your design is simple. Mentally block off a specific area—perhaps an area between two motifs. In that small area, draw a random wiggle or shape. Hook that line with one of your darkest or most unusual colors. Then hook on either side of the hooked line. Continue hooking on both sides until you fill the area or meet your motifs. Then move to another area and start the process again. Don't get sidetracked by looking at the entire rug; focus on only one small area at a time.

S Shape

S-shape hooking is the same as random, except that you use only S shapes—not all the same size, and not all in the same direction. Draw S shapes in different areas of the background with a Sharpie marker. Hook the S shape; then hook on both sides of the S shape. You'll end up with small areas to fill. This works great if you use at least three or four different values of

one color. Every once in a while, hook the S shape with darkest value and use the other values to fill in around it.

Hit and Miss

Hit and miss is frequently seen in antique hooked rugs, but it's normally used in the border, not the background. Hit and miss is a great way to use some of those cut strips left over from other projects. It can be done in straight or curved lines and should repeat colors and values used in the main design. For the best results, use plenty of neutrals and subdued colors in the hit-and-miss portion. If you use high-chroma colors, you may draw too much attention from the rug's main design, so use them only in short spurts here and there.

Mixtures

You can also use several of the previously mentioned techniques in the same rug. The background is your canvas. Hook the styles that you like, and make your rug individual. Use these different styles to enhance your design or motif. Primitive designs and motifs are usually simple and uncomplicated, giving you more leeway to have a more complicated or exciting background by using various textures and different hooking techniques. By using lots of textured fabrics in your background, you are also adding movement and interest.

BACKGROUND TIPS

To achieve the best results, consider the following factors when hooking the background.

If your design is simple, it's easier to use tweeds, textures, and various mottled colors more successfully. Don't try to balance each of the fabrics or colors—a random look is preferred. A simple design can easily carry a complicated background with many colors, textures, and hooking styles.

With a complicated or busy design or in a rug with little background area, it's best to keep the background simple. You can still use various tweeds or textures, but keep them closer in color and value than you might in a larger background.

Using a solid, non-textured fabric of one value for the background will make the rug look lifeless. Mottled fabrics and textured fabrics give the rug movement and life without making it too busy.

A busy background detracts from the beauty of a rug. Color, texture, and hooking style can all contribute to an overly busy background. A busy rug can easily become one that you never finish.

1885 Horses, 46" x 16". Hooked by Pat Freasier of Houston, Texas. This rug with a light background looks great, old, and finished, even though there is no border at all. (Printed by Woolley Fox in the *Keeping the Past Alive* series.)

It is easy to spot when the wrong background value has been used in a rug. It draws your eye away from the main design and can destroy a beautiful central motif. The perfect background value increases and supports the central motif.

A WORD ABOUT BORDERS

There are several schools of thought about borders: they frame or finish the rug, they add to the rug, they are necessary for the rug to be complete, they need to be darker than the majority of the rug, they can destroy a wonderful design, and on and on. But think of it this way: you don't normally pick out the frame before choosing a painting. The same is true with rug borders. Some rugs require a simple border or none at all; others can support an active or busy border with lots of colors and designs. Pictorials and geometrics look best with a simple border consisting of several rows of hooking that may repeat some of the colors in the main design. It's best to hook the design and some of the background before making a final decision on how to deal with the border.

Although most rugs look better with a border, not every rug needs one. By placing a solid piece of fabric on the outer border design, you can imagine your rug without a border. With primitives, the rug usually looks best with corners that are heavier, whether there is a border or not. That heaviness can be added simply by having dark motifs in the corners. The easiest way to get a heavier or weighted look is to use strong colors or dark values. In most cases, you need to be careful that the border doesn't become the main point of interest. But an overwhelming border in a primitive may be the perfect touch for that particular rug. If you look at antique rugs, you'll notice that there are many variations in the way borders are handled: some have nothing—they just sort of end, some have beautiful scrolls or floral arrangements, some have straight lines, some have hit-and-miss hooking. If you want your rug to have the look of an antique, let your border treatment develop as you're hooking the rug—let the rug lead you in the right direction. If you feel more comfortable preplanning your border, sketch your main design, make copies of it, and draw and color in several choices. One will most likely appeal to you more than the others.

CHAPTER 7

Specialty Fabrics

Rose Border, 34" x 45". This great old rug was probably made with old clothing. The entire background and border are made up of several gray fabrics. (From the Barbara Carroll Collection.)

Antique rugs were made with whatever fabrics the rug hookers had available. Consequently, most rugs were constructed of worn clothing consisting of a variety of fabrics, including silk, cotton, woven blankets, homespun fabrics, pieces of uniforms, rayon (also known as artificial silk,) yarn, stockings, satin, linen, velvet, wool, and paisley shawls. Remember, these rug hookers were creating utilitarian items—bed rugs for warmth or rugs to keep the cold air from coming through drafty wooden floors. They were not creating works of art to accent their homes' décor.

Luckily, we have access to an assortment of wonderful fabrics for rug hooking. Most of us prefer to use 100 percent wool fabric because it's hardwearing, longlasting, soft, and resilient, and most important, it has a tendency to repel dust and dirt. Sometimes I use 80 percent wool fabric if it provides the color or texture I want for a specific look. There is one wool fabric that I prefer not to use—worsted wool, which is most commonly found in men's suits. Because it is woven with the thread twisted, it tends to unravel as you're hooking. Worsted wool is also a thinner wool with a rough feel to it. I have been known to use a very small amount for an accent in the

Textured fabrics. *Textured* can mean a specific type of fabric, such as tweed, herringbone, or plaid, or it can simply mean that the wool has dimension—highs and lows or lumpy areas. Note that plaids and checks come in different sizes, each of which results in a different look in a rug. The purple would be either used sparingly or toned down with a wash for a primitive rug. The green and gold plaid is a Harris tweed purchased by a friend overseas.

perfect place, but it's not a fabric I would use in a large area. Some wools are thin and flimsy or rough and coarse; others are smooth and thick. Sometimes, the color or the value is more important than the thickness or quality of the wool.

To achieve a more authentic antique look, you can add other wools from recycled clothing, vintage woven woolen blankets, vintage fabrics, antique or vintage military uniforms, and antique paisley shawls. You can also use other fabrics, although good wool is the best and most long-lasting. Although cotton hooks up nicely and looks good initially, it gets dirty quickly and results in a more matted look. You may prefer to keep your cotton rugs off the floor and use them as wall hangings or tabletop pieces instead. But this is your rug, so feel free to use any fabrics you like.

RECYCLED FABRICS

Recycled fabric is just a fancy term for old clothing. Don't consider recycled wool as second rate or substandard. If it was good enough for our ancestors, it's good enough for us to mix in with our new wools. The best place to get recycled wool is your own closet, and you'll be giving discarded clothing a new life. Other

places to find recycled wool are donations from friends, garage sales, and thrift shops. The color and condition of the wool doesn't matter—not even if it's dirty or has moth holes or other damage. There is no such thing as an ugly wool, because it can always be overdyed or bled to make the color more appealing. The most important goal is to find 100 percent wool (although 80 percent can be used). If you're a beginner or a novice rug hooker, 100 percent wool is usually easier to hook with. Keep your eye open for tightly woven wool, which produces the best results, but don't pass up more loosely woven wool if it catches your eye and fits your color palette. The weave of recycled fabric will tighten and thicken when it's washed and dried.

You don't want to buy each and every piece of old wool clothing you find; be selective. The best pieces of old clothing to use for rug hooking are ladies' skirts and slacks. They are easy to take apart and yield the most fabric in large sections. Although men's jackets may have fabulous colors and textures, the amount of wool you recoup is seldom worth the effort. Normally, the only usable portions are the sleeves and the back of the jacket; the front, sides, and collar usually have a

These three new fabrics create the look of old or aged wool when hooked. The plaid with the distinctive sections works perfectly when hooked hit and miss for an antique rug, but you have to use some of each section—even the lightest one.

fusible facing that makes the fabric unusable for rug hooking. Pendleton wool shirts are a good investment, although it takes time and patience to take one apart. Depending on the size and style of the shirt, you'll get about two-thirds of a yard of usable wool. These shirts come in an array of colors and patterns that are most interesting when hooked. Stay away from the thinner or lightweight shirts; they won't tighten or thicken up enough when washed and dried. If you happen to come across pleated skirts or Scottish kilts, you've found a gold mine of high-quality wool. Especially with kilts, I take the time to remove the stitching of the pleats because of the large amount of wool it yields. You can find clothing in almost every solid color, but the pieces that are especially useful for creating the antique look are textured—plaids, tweeds, checks, herringbones, and heathers.

Recycling wool from old clothing to hook a rug is not only economical but also fun. Searching through garage sales and exploring thrift stores for those hidden treasures is a great way to spend a day. You may not find something every time, so be sure to make return trips. The best time of year to search is fall and winter. In early spring, although the supply may be limited, you might be lucky enough to find a thrift shop with greatly reduced prices.

Preparing Recycled Fabrics

All recycled clothing should be washed and dried before you expose it to your wool stash. These items may be dirty or, worse, they may contain moths or other bugs. Use a small amount of laundry detergent and warm water and run it through the wash cycle in your machine. When drying, use the permanent press cycle. If the wool fabric is already thick, you may want to line-dry it instead of using the dryer. It is *imperative* to clean your dryer's lint filter frequently.

Some people prefer to wash the items before taking them apart; others prefer to disassemble the clothing and discard the waste before washing and drying. I take the middle road. I cut away the waistband, pockets, and lining (outside my home) before washing and drying the fabric. After I remove it from the dryer, I take the items apart completely. Be sure to discard any worn areas. You'll recover more fabric if you take apart the seams, but I'm too impatient to do that. Instead, I make a snip with my scissors close to the seam and then simply tear the fabric so that I end up with the straight of the grain and the longest possible strips of wool from the garment.

You'll end up with many different sizes and pieces of fabric from recycled wool clothing. An easy way to store these irregular pieces is to first lay the largest piece flat and then layer smaller pieces on top of it. When you've finished layering one particular fabric, roll up the pieces and tie the bundle with a string or a strip of wool. The color and texture will still be easy to see, but the pieces will be neatly kept together.

Testing Recycled Wool

If there's no label and you're not sure whether the recycled fabric is 100 percent wool, there are several easy ways to test it.

Burn test. Cut a small, narrow triangle or sliver of fabric without any thread or seam stitching on it. Carefully light the narrower end with a match. Wool does not burn easily, smells like burning hair, and turns completely to soft ashes when rubbed between your fingers. If the fabric contains polyester, it will burn more easily and leave a hard, dark plastic bead; the larger the bead, the more polyester the fabric contains. If the fabric contains nylon, it will melt and leave a lighter-colored bead than polyester. Synthetics also flare more than wool when conducting the burn test. It's important to cut a sample that contains both horizontal and ver-

tical threads. If you pull just a few vertical threads and burn them, your results will be inconclusive at best or wrong at worst because you didn't test the horizontal threads, which could be polyester.

Bleach test. Cut two 1-inch squares of fabric. Pour 1 inch of bleach into a small jar, put one square of fabric in the jar, and cover it. Place the other cut square on top of the lid. Allow the fabric to soak overnight. If all the fabric disappears, it is wool. If there are threads still remaining, they indicate the percentage of man-made fabrics. If the entire square is still there, the piece is entirely synthetic.

Sound test. Cut a snip on a piece of known 100 percent wool fabric and tear it. Listen to the smooth sound it makes. Then cut a snip on a piece of known polyester-wool blend and tear it. Notice the crackling, rough sound it makes when torn. Now you can tear any questionable fabric and determine whether it contains any polyester by listening to the sound it makes.

Touch test. Some people have the ability to tell the makeup of a fabric by rubbing it against their skin. If it feels soft, it's wool; if it has a scratchy feeling, it has some man-made fibers in it. I consider this the least reliable test, because I have been fooled.

Textured pieces of wool; some are designer pieces, and some must be cut with scissors.

VINTAGE FABRICS

Besides recycled clothing, there are many other wonderful items that can be used. Vintage woven woolen blankets can be found at garage sales or thrift shops. The best blankets for rug hooking are of medium weight. Because the weave will tighten and thicken when washed and dried, ignore the heavier blankets. Occasionally, I line-dry a blanket to keep it from getting too thick and dense to hook. When I first started rug hooking, the rule of thumb was to cut thicker fabric on a narrower strip so that it would be similar to the other cuts used. But for the antique style, we relish the fact that the thicker wool creates a wider strip and gives the rug a more varied look. These blankets can also be overdyed, so don't ignore those with moth holes, stains, or weird patterns.

Using vintage clothes is another way to give your rug an antique look. One of the best and most easily obtained type of vintage clothing is military uniforms, especially army greens. Some rug hookers think the color is ugly, but it is actually one of the most perfect colors for the antique look. Furthermore, don't pass up

any old woolen scarves, regardless of the patterns or colors. They may need to be toned down or muted, but you can easily do that by using the complementary color.

My favorite fabric for achieving an antique look is antique paisley shawls. In the early 1980s I started collecting shawls that were produced mainly from 1830 to 1880. These shawls are called paisleys not because of the design but because so many of them were produced in Paisley, Scotland—first by hand-drawn looms, and later by Jacquard looms. (For more information on paisley shawls, see the September/October 2004 issue of *Rug Hooking*.) My collection includes many museum-quality shawls that I intend to preserve for future generations to enjoy. But I've also purchased shawls that were well past the point of repair or restoration. Millions of these paisleys were manufactured in Scotland, England, and France and can still be found at garage sales and antique shops. Please, don't even think about cutting apart a shawl in good condition or one with an usual color or design (paisleys were made in many colors—not just the most common orange). Even if it's damaged, have someone knowledgeable

Paisley Hearts, 24" x 30". Designed and hooked by Cynthia Norwood. All the motifs in this rug were done in antique paisleys. Paisleys can be found in green, purple, and rose, as well as the more common orange, gold, and red. Note the use of bright orange only in the star. The medium-value gray background, made entirely of recycled wool, tones down the brightness of the paisleys. The border fabric is a wool that works well with paisley. New wool was used only on the border and the finished edge.

These two fabrics closely replicate the look of antique paisley shawls if you can't bring yourself to use the real thing.

take a look at it before you cut it into pieces. It may be worth preserving.

The look you get from antique paisley shawls can't be duplicated with hand-dyed wool or even textured fabrics. A few fabrics can produce a similar effect, but they don't have the life that a paisley has. Before cutting a paisley, examine both sides carefully. You'll notice that the correct side is tightly woven, while the reverse side is sort of thready. Note which way the threads run, because you want to cut the paisley in the same direction. If you cut across the long threads, the wool will simply shred into nothing. Tear a strip of paisley less than 4 inches wide and about 18 inches long if you're using a mechanical cutter to make the strips. This narrower piece will help you stay on the straight of the grain. If you get off the straight of the grain, the paisley will shred. Cuts #7 and wider can be made easily with a cutter. If you want a narrower strip, you can cut a wide strip and fold it in half lengthwise when hooking. Some paisleys are woven tightly enough that they can be cut as narrow as a #4 or #5 cut. Test your piece of paisley before cutting it to determine the best width. I generally prefer to cut paisley by hand with scissors; I find it relaxing, and it puts me in the mind-set of rug hookers from

the late 1800s or early 1900s. I recommend that you cut only a small amount at a time, whether you're using a cutter or a pair of scissors. Paisley is not inexpensive or in endless supply. The less you cut at one time, the less you'll waste.

Paisley leaves threads on the back of your hooking. You can trim these if you want to, but it's not necessary; I just leave them alone. When hooking with paisley, you'll find that you need to fill more holes of the backing than you do with 100 percent wool. This is because the paisley is thinner than modern wool. You can hook paisley with the right side up or with the reverse side showing, but the right side wears much better. Because paisley is so expensive and hard to find, most people use it only as an accent or to outline items. You may, however, fall in love with the look and want to put some paisley in every piece you hook.

FASHION OR DESIGNER FABRICS

Another group of wools, called fashion or designer fabrics, is much more expensive and sometimes harder to use. However, they are clearly not your normal, run-of-the-mill fabrics. If they are priced too high for your budget, just use them for sparkle or interest or to outline, rather than hooking a large area with them. Some of these fabrics won't tear and must be hand-cut with scissors, but the result is well worth the effort. Specialty woven wools, such as Harris tweeds from England, and fabrics such as boucle come very close to duplicating the antique look. Keep your eyes open for out-of-the-ordinary wools to make your rug special.

The most important thing to remember when deciding which fabrics to use is that this is your rug. Make your own choices, and don't worry about explaining them to others. Feel confident enough to use any fabric you want—velour, suede, knits, and cottons, as well as wools. I have no problem putting all my rugs on the floor, regardless of the fabric I use. Even those with a lot of paisley are placed in high-traffic areas. The wear only helps them look older and better.

CHAPTER 8

Finishing Methods

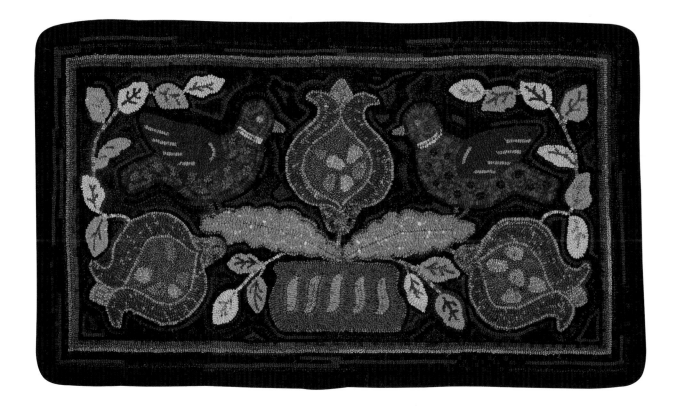

Birds and Pomegranates, 41" x 24". Designed by Edith O'Neill. Hooked by Janet Griffith of Frisco, Texas. Note the fabulous use of different values in the background, the three different colors in the pods of the pomegranates, the golden leaves, and the red and purple birds. Aren't they great?

O ne of the most important aspects of hooking a rug is the finishing method used. A poorly finished rug is akin to getting all dressed up and then going out with dirty, bare feet. Some rug hookers spend hours designing, dyeing, and hooking their rugs but then haphazardly finish the edges or binding. Since there are many methods to choose from, I suggest that you examine the bindings of every rug you see. You'll notice that one method may look good with fine hooked pieces, while another method better complements more primitive rugs. Techniques vary in terms of ease and time to complete, but chances are that you'll find one method that appeals to you.

THE IMPORTANCE OF STEAMING

Whichever finishing method you choose, the hooked piece needs to be steamed (this is sometimes referred to as blocking, but it's not as tedious as blocking a piece of needlepoint). Steaming makes the rug look smooth and causes uneven loops to appear more uniform. This step is especially important when you've used strips of different widths and different thicknesses of wool. There are different schools of thought on steaming: Some steam only the reverse side of the hooking, some steam first the back and then the front, and some steam only the front side. Some people put a wet towel under the hooking as well as on top of it. Some steam their rugs after completing the binding or finishing edges, rather than before. I haven't discovered

Indian Peace Flag, 39" x 31". Hooked by Billie Jean Glass of Lexington, Kentucky. Only five of these historic flags are known to exist. The fourteenth star is thought to be for Vermont. The flag was given to the Indians in a show of peace. Billie Jean has used wonderful textured wools to re-create the aged look of a flag. (Printed by Woolley Fox in the Keeping the Past Alive series.)

any difference in terms of which side you steam, but I do prefer steaming the rug before finishing the edges. Feel free to use whichever method you wish.

Steaming the rug before finishing the edges makes the rug more pliable and easier to handle while finishing. It's a good idea to steam your rug on a piece of scrap carpet, because some color may bleed through. Alternatively, you can place some old sheets or towels under the rug. I steam my rugs on a large counter that's about waist high. It's nice to be able to stand during the steaming process, because although it's simple, it's not fast. My preference is to steam on the right side of the rug, and I usually steam only once. However, if this is your first primitive rug, you'll probably need to steam it more than once.

Begin the steaming process by placing your rug in an area where it won't be disturbed until both the rug and its foundation are dry. Completely wet a towel and wring out most of the water. It should be thoroughly saturated, but not so wet that it's dripping water on the floor. Don't use either a new fluffy towel or one that's completely worn out. And don't use one of your good towels, because it might get stained or discolored. It's not necessary to use an oversize bath towel; you can simply rewet a hand towel or smaller bath towel as needed. I have one towel that I've used exclusively for steaming for years.

Place the wet towel directly on top of the hooked rug. I like to start steaming in the middle of the rug, but it's not necessary to do so. Set your iron to high heat, and place it in the center of the rug, directly on top of the towel. You need not apply any pressure or move the iron around; just let it sit in place for up to 10 seconds. It will produce plenty of steam, but it won't burn the rug. After 10 seconds, lift the iron, move it a short distance so that the iron overlaps the steamed area, and once again leave it on for about 10 seconds. Rewet the towel as needed. Continue this process until you have steamed the entire rug. Remove the damp towel. Don't move the rug until it is dry.

HISTORICAL METHODS OF FINISHING

Some finishing methods that were used in the past are not recommended. For example, our ancestors often just folded the edge under and hooked through two layers of burlap up to the edge of the burlap. Thus, the finished edge was hooked, and no cord, binding, or whipping was used to protect the edges. Although this method is easy, it also has the shortest life span and is very difficult to repair. Another option— not much better than the first—was to hook the rug, trim the burlap, turn the burlap edge under, and slip-stitch it to the backside of the hooking.

Stubbs Runner, 48" x 20". Hooked by Barbara Carroll. This great rug is full of fun and whimsy. The border is a collection of wools made up of lights, mediums, and darks in different colors and textures. The medium background gives the rug an instant aged look. (Printed by Woolley Fox in the Keeping the Past Alive series.)

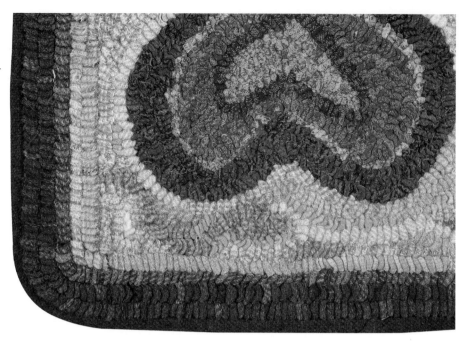

The corner of a Paisley Hearts rug shows how to use wool fabric to cover the backing—my favorite finishing method for primitive rugs.

CURRENT RECOMMENDATIONS

Many rug hookers use rug binding tape (1^1/$_4$ inches wide and made of cotton) for the finished edge. Some sew the tape on by machine before hooking the rug, but this limits the size of your rug because it's not easy to remove if you happen to change your mind. Some people also wash and press the rug tape before attaching it, based on the fact that it's made of cotton and might shrink. I omit this step because there's no way my rug will ever be in water hot enough to shrink the tape.

When I use rug-binding tape, I sew it on after hooking the rug. The only exception is if I'm hooking a round chair seat pad for a specific chair. Then I sew the tape on first, hook right up to the tape, trim the excess foundation, and stitch the tape down. For a rug, you can zigzag the foundation about 1 inch beyond the hooking. Then hand-sew or machine-stitch the rug tape onto the backing, getting it as close as possible to the loops. Trim the excess backing, and turn the tape and backing under together. Blind-stitch the tape loosely to the hooked foundation, taking care to make sure the excess backing is covered. You can place a piece of cording between the hooking and the rug tape to give the edge a little more protection. Steam the edges for a nice finished look.

You can also use rug-binding tape with a whipped yarn edge. I prefer 100 percent wool tapestry yarn when whipping, but it's most important to choose the same color as the last row of hooking. After you complete the hooking, zigzag about 1^1/$_2$ inches from the edge of the hooking. Trim the excess foundation. Place thin cording on the back side of the backing, and turn the backing under. About ^{1}/$_4$ inch of the backing will be visible on the right side of the rug. With yarn, whip or overcast this edge. Hide the yarn tails; do not make knots. The normal finished width of this whipped edge is ^{3}/$_4$ inch, but you can make it wider by using wider cording. The corners need to be slowly shaped with yarn. Then cover the remaining backing on the back side with rug binding tape. Stitch the tape by hand as close as you can to the whipped edge, and stitch it down loosely on the foundation. For an easy and unusual way of attaching the yarn and tape at the same time, see *Secrets of Primitive Hooked Rugs* or *American Folk Art Rug Hooking*, both by Barbara Carroll.

MY FAVORITE FINISHING METHODS

There are three methods that I like to use, depending on the type of rug I'm hooking: whipped edge without rug tape,

Hannah's Barnyard, showing a corner edge with #8-cut wool strips covering the linen backing. (Designed and hooked by Cynthia Norwood.)

Comstock, 35" x 37". Hooked Anita White of Overland, Kansas. This fabulous antique pattern was printed by Lib Callaway. Anita did a great job using soft, muted colors and moving them around this rug. Touches of paisley here and there are an added benefit, and her finishing is exquisite.

wool fabric binding, or cut wool strips for edging.

The whipped edge without rug tape works well with rugs hooked with fine- or medium-cut widths of wool, but it can be used with primitive rugs as well. After you hook the rug, zigzag or stitch two rows of straight stitches about 1¹/₂ inches from the last row of hooking. Trim the excess foundation or backing. (If you don't have access to a sewing machine, don't trim all the excess foundation at once. Trim only a few inches at a time. This will keep the foundation from unraveling while you're working on it.) The next step is to double-fold or double-roll the foundation, which means folding the foundation in half and then folding it in half again. With this method, it's not necessary to add cording. You can stitch this roll with needle and thread to keep it in place. Then whip or overcast the rolled edge with yarn, taking care to bring the yarn up as close as possible to the row of loops. There is no backing showing, and no rug tape is necessary. The look is clean and crisp, and your eye isn't distracted by mismatched tape.

For more primitive rugs, I prefer to use wool fabric—either cut wool strips or fabric binding. Using wool fabric as binding is the easiest and quickest method When using this method, I also double-fold the $1^1/2$ inches of remaining foundation, just as I do for the whipped edge without tape. You don't have to cut the wool on the bias. Simply tear wool up to 2 inches wide, either with or against the grain. I use the direction that gives me the most length. You may need to sew a couple of strips together to achieve sufficient length to go around the perimeter of the rug. Mitering those pieces makes the binding smoother and more uniform. This leaves you with two torn edges of wool fabric. It isn't necessary to straight-stitch or zigzag either edge. Push one torn edge as close as you can to the last row of hooking. With needle and thread, stitch it down to the foundation. I like to take a couple of stitches and then do one backstitch. The shorter the needle, the smaller and tighter your stitches will be. Then turn the wool fabric under the rug, around the rolled or double-folded edge. You can turn the raw torn edge under before stitching it down, or you can stitch down the raw edge. You need to use a tightly woven wool when employing this method. For a more unusual look, cut the wool on the bias, if your wool to textured or patterned.

One advantage to using wool strips is that you're depleting your pile of leftover strips. When using this method, I double-

roll or -fold the remaining foundation and stitch it in place. The strips work best if they are #8-cut and made of tightly woven wool. Use your hook (or a wide-eyed needle) to pull the wool strips through the foundation as close as possible to the last row of hoops. Don't allow the wool strips to twist or roll. You can either place the whipped strips of wool next to each other or overlap them a bit. When you get close to the end of the wool strip, place it on a wide-eyed needle and hide the tail under the whipped edge. The finished look is nice, and you don't need rug-binding tape.

There are many other methods of finishing the edges of a rug. Talk to instructors, read books, and look at other rugs to find the one you like best. But whichever method you choose, take the time to do it well. It is sad to see a wonderfully hooked rug with shoddy or careless finished edges. It may be necessary to steam the edges of the rug when completed.

When hooking a rug, I take one step that makes the finishing a little easier. Instead of hooking square corners, I slightly round the last two rows of hooking. This means that I don't have to worry about mitering the corners when completing the finished edges. When the rug is finished and displayed, no one will notice that the corners aren't square.

LABELING

After you finish the edges of your rug, please take the time to make a label for it. This is a work of art, and it should be signed. It is essential to include your name and the date, and it would be nice for future generations if you also included the name of the rug and its designer. Add any other important information, especially if the rug was made for a special event or person. The label can be as simple as using a laundry marker on muslin or as fancy as a one-of-a-kind label that is cross-stitched and hand-sewn to the back of the rug.

CHAPTER 9

Dyeing Techniques for an Antique Look

Dyeing can be a challenge, but there are several simple techniques that provide fantastic results and wonderful antique-looking wools. These methods are perfect for beginning rug hookers or those with no experience in fabric dyeing. After you have experimented with these basic dyeing techniques, advance to dyeing with chemical dyes.

BASIC GUIDELINES

Whether you're using natural products of chemical dyes, you should follow these basic guidelines.

Safety. Safety should be your primary concern. Be sure to use caution and common sense around hot water, steam, and dyes. One steam burn will teach you the importance of keeping burn ointment on hand. I have an aloe vera plant in my dye area—the juice of the leaf is a

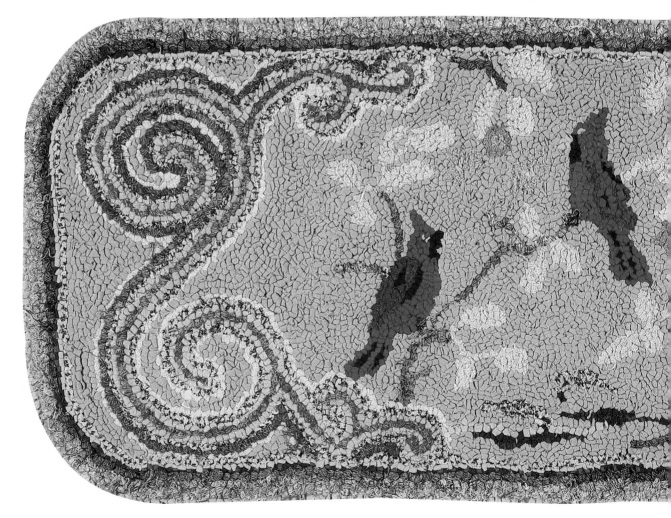

natural remedy for minor burns. Also, keep extra towels nearby to clean up spills. Always wear gloves. I prefer Bluettes (available in hardware stores), which are thick blue gloves with a cotton liner; when wearing them, you can actually put your hands directly in simmering water. Buy the gloves a size larger than your hands so they slip on and off easily. Set aside certain containers that will be used only for dyeing. Label them and keep them separate from cooking utensils. Never use these containers for food preparation. Safety glasses and a mask are other useful precautions.

Records. Keep a dye book, where you make notes and save samples. Note whether or not you like a particular method or formula. Glue a small sample in the book next to each formula—from both before and after dyeing. You may not be able to exactly match a piece of wool, but having notes to refer to will allow you to get much closer to the original without so much trial and error.

Treatment of wool. It's best to start with wet wool for most techniques. You can presoak it overnight in dish-washing detergent, or use a wetting agent such as Synthrapol (PROChem) for immediate use. This step allows the dye to permeate all the fibers and avoids leaving a white line running through the piece of cut wool. Never boil the wool; simmer only. The water should be boiling only as you add the wool. Less water and less stirring create more mottled pieces of wool. More water and more stirring create more uniformly dyed wool. Keep in mind that wool will dry at least one shade lighter than when wet. Rinse dyed wool with gradually cooling water. Don't shock the wool. When drying wool in the dryer, clean the lint filter frequently. If the color bleeds when rinsing the wool, put it in a vinegar bath (mixture of water

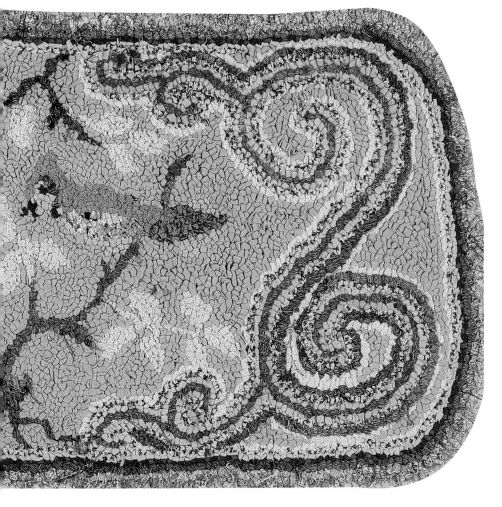

Birds on Branch, 48" x 19". This rug, hooked entirely with as-is clothing or fabrics—proves that you don't have to dye to create a great rug. The solitary blue jay breaks all the rules, but it makes you smile. The simple scroll is very effective, and note, the single golden orange line around the border. Imagine what this rug hooker could have done with walnut hulls or onion skins! (From the author's collection.)

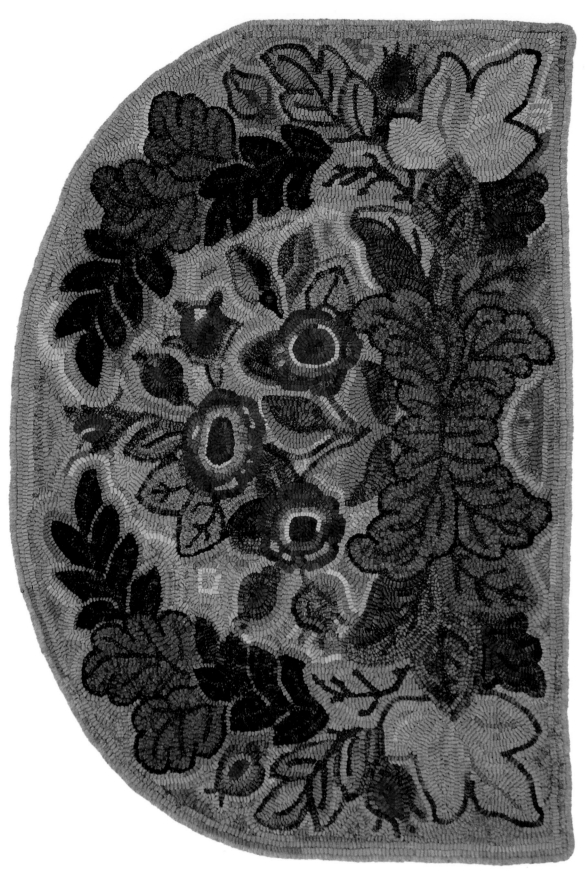

Early Threshold, 37" x 26". Hooked by Cindy Trick of Beavercreek, Ohio, with a #8-cut on linen. Note how the background, dyed with onionskins, softens this rug. Cindy captured the personality of the old florals—very Victorian. (Copyright Heirloom Rugs. Photographed by Larry Bosely, Encore Production Services, Cincinnati, Ohio.)

and vinegar) and simmer for a few more minutes.

Time. Don't try to rush the dyeing process. Choose a time when you won't be interrupted, and let the answering machine pick up any calls. It takes a specific amount of time and a sufficient degree of temperature to develop certain colors. Failure to let the dye set (that is, to make the color permanent, so it won't run or bleed) will cause problems later when you steam the finished rug. At that point, having a color run onto a neighboring wool can break your heart.

Color wheel. Buy and use a color wheel. There are many different types on the market, from the cheap to the very expensive. Purchase whatever kind you like, but make sure you understand how it works and get comfortable using it.

ONION SKINS

Using onion skins is one of the easiest ways to get muted, antique-looking colors; they can be used over any color fabric—solid or textured. The most visible result is obtained on white or natural fabrics. There are many different ways to use onion skins, and each dyer has a favorite technique.

Onion skins are easily obtained. You can simply go to a grocery store and pick them from the produce bin; add an onion to the plastic bag, and pay on the way out. Or talk to the produce manager and ask that they save the skins for you after cleaning the onions. To get a golden look, use yellow onion skins. Red or purple onion skins result in a more beige color. You can mix the skins together or use only one color at a time. Don't waste your time with white onion skins, though; the results are minimal.

Put the onion skins (one type or mixed) in a pot with water and simmer. The more water you use, the more diluted the mixture will be. Simmer for 20 minutes or more. Make sure to watch the pot so it doesn't burn; you may need to add water occasionally. You can either use the resulting solution immediately or save it for later. If you want to store it, let the mixture cool, and drain the liquid into a jar that can be sealed. Alternatively, you can put the liquid into ice trays and freeze it until needed. Throw the skins away, or simmer them again to make more of the solution. The stored solution will have to be reheated before using it.

Either put the onion skin solution directly on pieces of wool, or add the solution to a pot of simmering water on top of the stove. Put your wet wool in the pot, and let it simmer for 15 minutes. Pour in more onion skin solution if desired. Add several tablespoons of vinegar to the pot, and allow the contents to simmer for 15 more minutes, or until the water clears. If the fabric is bleeding color, you may need to add more vinegar and simmer longer. You can rinse the fabric starting with warm water and then gradually cooler water, or you can let the wool cool and then rinse it.

Another method is to place the onion skins themselves directly on the wool. Place wet wool in a pan; the wool can be smoothed out, accordion folded, or haphazardly placed, and you can include fabrics of different colors if you like. If you want the onion skin dyeing to be very strong, presoak the wool in vinegar, and don't rinse it out. For a more mottled, less harsh result, don't presoak in vinegar. Place a layer of dry or wet onion skins directly on the fabric, and sprinkle non-iodized salt over the skins. Add another layer of fabric, onion skins, and salt. Repeat for as many layers as your pan can hold. To one of the corners of the pan, add a small amount of water with couple tablespoons of vinegar. Cover the pan with foil, but be sure to tent the foil (if the foil touches dark wool, a reaction between them will leave a white stain). Bake for at least 30 minutes at 300 degrees or less.

Be very careful when removing the pan from the oven. Let it cool before lifting the foil, because it will be filled with steam. Always open the side of the foil farthest away from your body. Carefully rinse to remove the onion skins. If the wool is bleeding color as you're rinsing, you may need to add more vinegar and

Carolyn's Hearth, 66" x 36". Hooked by Jenny Rupp of West Chester, Ohio, with a #8 cut on burlap. This simple but wonderful design is accented by the color flow. This look is representative of fabrics overdyed with walnut hulls—they have a warm glow. (Copyright Heirloom Rugs. Photographed by Larry Bosley, Encore Production Services, Cincinnati, Ohio.)

bake or simmer on the stove top for another 20 minutes or so.

WALNUT HULLS

Another natural dye that produces great results is black walnut hulls. Simmer black walnuts—whole or cracked—in a pot of water. Choose a pot that you don't intend to use for food, because it will be permanently stained. The less water you use, the stronger the dye solution will be. The solution can be stored in a sealed jar or frozen, but it must be stirred and heated when you're ready to use it. An easier and faster way to get the same effect is to buy crushed black walnut hulls crystals (Fredericksburg Rugs) and simmer down the solution. This dye solution can be used in the same way as the onion skin solution. My advice is to start with a small amount and gradually add more if desired. This solution can be used to make wonderfully aged off-white fabrics or to tone down colored fabrics. I hooked a geometric rug using all as-is recycled wool that had been overdyed with a walnut hull wash. The result was a soft rug, because all the fabrics had a common base.

If you require stronger areas of dark brown, presoak the fabric in vinegar. Squeeze out most of the vinegar, but don't rinse. Put the wool in a pot with a small amount of water, and place the whole or cracked walnuts or the walnut crystals directly on the fabric. Let this simmer for at least 20 minutes. When the wool has absorbed enough stain, either remove the walnut completely or move it to a new spot. Add vinegar and water if needed. Simmer another 20 minutes, or until the water is clear. Cool and rinse the wool.

Other natural products can be used for dyeing in the same way. For example, you can get beautiful flesh-colored wool from avocado pits using the walnut hull method. Experiment and have fun. But don't waste your time with pecan hulls and garlic skins—I learned that from experience.

MARRYING OR STEWING FABRICS

Another easy technique for novices is to marry fabrics. Put pieces of various wet or dry fabrics in a pot of warm water with 1 teaspoon baking soda. Simmer uncovered for 30 minutes, keeping an eye on the pot so it doesn't boil over. As the fabrics simmer, color seeps out of them. The next step is to add vinegar—but make sure the pot is large enough to accommodate the bubbles from the chemical reaction produced by mixing baking soda and vinegar. Simmer until the water is clear. Rinse the wool until the water clears. The resulting colors are more muted than the original, and these wools can easily be used in one rug. You can also add some onion skin or walnut hull solution to some of the wools for another look.

You can get a nice assortment of background wools by taking various dark fabrics and marrying them. This works best if one of the colors bleeds more than the

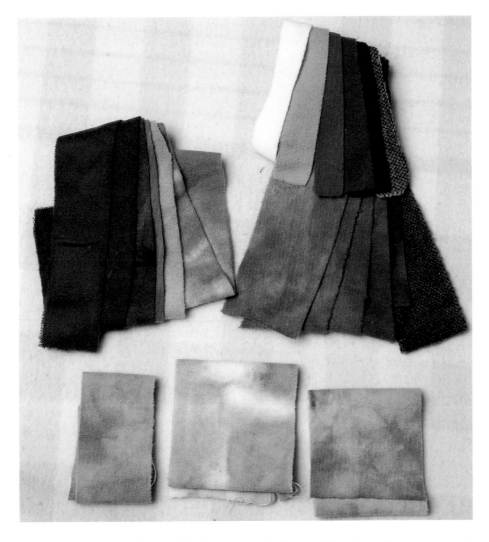

Samples of dyeing for nondyers. Clockwise from the top right: In the group of browns, the fabrics on top were married to get the beautiful browns underneath; no dye was added. Next is a natural-color fabric dyed with walnut hulls. The center piece on the bottom was dyed using onion skins. The piece on the left was dyed with tea bags. In the group of fabrics on the top left, the original fabric was green; color was bled from it, resulting in the golden piece. The "blood" was then used to overdye natural wool blue.

rest. If not, you can always add a bright piece of fabric to the kettle for some punch. You should end up with enough wool for a wonderfully interesting dark background. Conversely, if you have several whites and light-textured fabrics, you can add a small piece of a darker fabric to tone down the brightness or whiteness of the original fabrics.

Another option is to take a very bright or high-chroma piece of wool and place it in a pot with some dark wools. The bright piece will end up being toned down and muted, making it perfect for the antique look. When using this process, you can consult a color wheel to predict the results. Use the complementary color—the one directly opposite on the color wheel—to tone down a piece of fabric. For instance, if you have a piece of very bright yellow, you can tone it down by simmering it with a small piece of pur-

ple fabric. When the yellow is as muted as you want it, remove it from the pot and place it in a fresh pot with water and vinegar to simmer for 20 minutes. Always save a piece of the original fabric as a control piece, so you can compare it and see how much the fabric in the pot is changing.

When marrying wools, you can use several from the same color family—such as lime green, emerald green, and olive green—that you normally wouldn't even consider putting together in a rug. Once they're married, however, it's a different story. Upon completion of the process, these wools will be more similar to one another and can work together beautifully in a rug. You can also marry several different colors; although the colors won't change completely, they will acquire some of the "blood" from the other fabrics and thus be related enough to use in one rug.

Cynthia's Favorite Dye Formulas

FOUR EASY LIGHT BACKGROUNDS

Light #1	Light #2	Light #3	Light #4
$1/4$ tsp seal brown	$1/4$ tsp golden brown	$1/4$ tsp mahogany	$1/16$ tsp black
$1/4$ tsp khaki drab	$1/32$ tsp black	$1/16$ tsp black	$1/4$ tsp spice brown

FOUR EASY DARK BACKGROUNDS

Dark #1	Dark #2	Dark #3	Dark #4
$1/4$ tsp blue	$1/4$ tsp black	$1/4$ tsp silver-gray green	$1/4$ tsp black
$1/16$ tsp black	$1/16$ tsp peacock	$1/4$ tsp khaki drab	$1/4$ tsp reseda green

FAVORITE COLORS

Gold	**Olive Green**
$1/8$ tsp old gold	$1/4$ tsp bright green
$1/32$ tsp golden brown	$1/32$ tsp terra cotta
Rich Red	**Rich Blue**
$1/4$ tsp crimson	$1/4$ tsp blue
$1/16$ tsp terra cotta	$1/16$ tsp old gold
Rusty Brown	**Favorite Green**
$1/16$ tsp orange	$1/4$ tsp olive green
$1/32$ tsp terra cotta	$1/4$ tsp hunter green
Antique Mahogany	**Fake Onion Skin**
1 tsp mahogany	$1/4$ tsp ecru
$1/2$ tsp dark brown	$1/4$ tsp old ivory
$1/16$ tsp bronze green	$1/4$ tsp champagne
Grunge Green	**Old Splatterware**
$1/2$ tsp khaki drab	$1/2$ tsp navy blue
$1/16$ tsp golden brown	$1/2$ tsp Copenhagen blue
$1/16$ tsp woodrose	$1/16$ tsp silver gray
$1/32$ tsp old gold	$1/4$ tsp peacock

Some call this process stewing when different colors of wool are used.

REMOVING COLOR

This technique is always unpredictable and loads of fun. It's impossible to look at a piece of wool and be sure what color will bleed from it or what color the fabric will end up being. For instance, you can bleed or remove color from olive fabric and get blue blood, and the original olive green fabric may end up being teal, brown, or gold. Therefore, the best advice is to test small pieces of wool, one at a time, to see what the results are. Then, if you're happy with the results, you can use a larger piece of fabric. You can use the blood from the wool as if it were a chemical dye, soak it back into the original piece of wool, or simply throw it away.

To get started, put a small piece of wool in a pan of simmering water. Put in a few drops of baby shampoo—Johnson's works best. Color should start seeping out shortly. Let the wool simmer. The longer it simmers, the more color will escape. If you want the wool to become a lighter shade, place it in clean water and add more shampoo. When the wool becomes the shade or color you like, remove it from the pot and place it in a fresh pot of simmering water. Add several tablespoons of vinegar and simmer for 20 minutes, or until the water clears. The blood can be used immediately on another piece of fabric. To do so, simmer for at least 20 minutes, add vinegar, and simmer until clear. When dyeing with the blood, you won't get rich, dark colors, but it adds life to some fabrics and is great over light-colored wools.

The longest I ever simmered a piece of wool was 40 minutes. If it doesn't bleed color in 10 minutes, it probably won't. Browns are notorious for not bleeding. You can bleed textured fabrics as well as solid fabrics. If you have a bright, bold plaid, bleeding it and then adding vinegar will pull the colors back into the fabric, but in a more muted, mottled way.

Instead of baby shampoo, you can use baking soda to remove color or get blood from a fabric. Just remember to use a pan large enough for the bubbles caused by mixing baking soda with vinegar. Color can also be removed with hot water in your kitchen sink. Fill the sink with hot water, and add $2/3$ cup Arm and Hammer washing soda (without bleach). Add the wool, and soak it for at least 1 hour. Drain the water and rinse the wool. If you want to remove even more color, refill the sink with hot water, add more washing soda, soak the wet wool for another hour, and rinse well. If not, remove the wool from the sink and simmer it in a large pot with vinegar, or put the wool in a pan of vinegar water, tent it with foil, and bake it at 300 degrees for 45 minutes. Then cool and rinse the wool until the water clears. If the water doesn't clear, you may have to repeat the process in the oven or on the stove top.

CHEMICAL DYES

Human beings have been interested in creating and controlling color since ancient times. Luckily, we no longer need to collect and crush cochineal insects for red dye or shellfish for purple dye. Chemical dyes became more prominent in the mid-1800s, and we now have a wide assortment of easy-to-use dyes. So when you want a specific color that you can't find seem to find anywhere, why not be adventuresome and try something a little more complicated than the simple dyeing techniques described earlier? Don't miss out on the excitement of creating your own wonderful colors and having unlimited control over color selection.

There are many good dye books on the market, but there are two that I highly recommend: *Antique Colours for Primitive Rugs* by Barbara Carroll and Emma Lou Lais (which provides formulas using Cushing dyes) and *Beautiful Wool: A Hand-Dyers Guide* by Laurice Heath (which uses both Cushing and PRO-Chem dyes). Both have wonderful color photos of dyed samples and good, easy-to-follow directions, and both have great dye formulas for antique-looking rugs. These books were written by people who hook primitive rugs, so they understand the colors and shades we're looking for. Two other booklets that use PROChem Wash-Fast acid dyes to create great antique-looking colors are the Society for the Preservation of New England Antiquities' *Historic Colors of America* by Sharon Townsend, and Holly Hill Designs' *Dyeing for Color* by Susan Quicksall. These booklets don't have color photos of dyed samples, however.

Although there is no one correct way to dye, you should follow the author's directions, because each dyer uses different techniques that may affect the outcome. Dyeing is a lot like cooking. We all have our own recipes and way of doing things. Don't try to learn several methods at once; after you become proficient with one method of dyeing, try another. Don't be afraid of making a mistake, because there is no such thing; you may end up with a piece of fabric that didn't turn out the way you expected, but it may be perfect for another project or for another person. Think of dyeing as an art, not a science. Have fun and experiment with your wool.

Dyeing Tips

Remember to always add boiling water to dry dye—not the other way around. If you make the mistake of adding dry dye to a cup of boiling water, you may have a mild explosion and quite a mess to clean up. Start with dry dye crystals in a container. Add boiling water to the container; you now have a liquid dye solution. After adding the boiling water to the dry dye, mix it well and then let it rest for couple minutes before using it. On the stovetop, bring water to a boil in a large enough container to hold the desired amount of wool. Add the premixed dye solution. Always start by adding a small amount of dry solution; you can always add more to get a darker shade. Add the wet, pre-soaked wool. Simmer the wool for at least 20 minutes. Stir, add vinegar, and simmer another 20 minutes, or until the water clears. Let the dyed wool cool, and then rinse it. I put dyed wool of similar colors in the washer and run the rinse and spin cycles; then I dry the wool in the dryer on permanent press (clean the lint filter after each load).

The amount of fabric you use determines whether the resulting shade will be light, medium, or dark. The more wool you use, the lighter the color will be; the less wool you use, the darker the color will be. The amount of water in the dye pot doesn't affect the color, but the more water you have in the pot, the freer the wool is to move around, and the more uniform the dye results will be. If you want a more mottled result, simply use less water to crowd the wool in the dye pot.

Water is one of the unknowns when dyeing. Two people can dye the same formula over the same fabric and get dissimilar results, depending on the chemicals in their water. They may live a few blocks apart or miles apart, have well water or city water. If it's important to get consistent results every time, use distilled water. For primitive rugs, however, we don't have to be that precise or particular.

My Favorite Dye Formulas

Although I now dye by eye and no longer use formulas, a few of my favorites (using Cushing dyes) devised after years of experimentation can be seen on page 68. I use TOD spoons and Grey spoons to measure the dry dye. Put the dry dye in a container, add 1 cup of boiling water, stir well, let the dye mixture rest a couple of minutes. Add fabric to the pot of boiling water with the amount of dye mixture desired. More of the liquid solution will result in a darker color. That's why it's best to begin with a small amount of the liquid dye mixture and to add more water.